Th

-

DODO PRESS

CONTENTS

# The Common People of Ancient Rome

## Studies of Roman Life and Literature

By

Frank Frost Abbott

## Prefatory Note

This book, like the volume on "Society and Politics in Ancient Rome," deals with the life of the common people, with their language and literature, their occupations and amusements, and with their social, political, and economic conditions. We are interested in the common people of Rome because they made the Roman Empire what it was. They carried the Roman standards to the Euphrates and the Atlantic; they lived abroad as traders, farmers, and soldiers to hold and Romanize the provinces, or they stayed at home, working as carpenters, masons, or bakers, to supply the daily needs of the capital.

The other side of the subject which has engaged the attention of the author in studying these topics has been the many points of similarity which arise between ancient and modern conditions, and between the problems which the Roman faced and those which confront us. What policy shall the government adopt toward corporations? How can the cost of living be kept down? What effect have private benefactions on the character of a people? Shall a nation try to introduce its own language into the territory of a subject people, or shall it allow the native language to be used, and, if it seeks to introduce its own tongue, how can it best accomplish its object? The Roman attacked all these questions, solved some of them admirably, and failed with others egregiously. His successes and his failures are perhaps equally illuminating, and the fact that his attempts to improve social and economic conditions run through a period of a thousand years should make the study of them of the greater interest and value to us.

Of the chapters which this book contains, the article on "The Origin of the Realistic Romance among the Romans" appeared originally in *Classical Philology*, and the author is indebted to the editors of that periodical for permission to reprint it here. The other papers are now published for the first time.

It has not seemed advisable to refer to the sources to substantiate every opinion which has been expressed, but a few references have been given in the foot-notes mainly for the sake of the reader who may wish to follow some subject farther than has been possible in these brief chapters. The proofs had to be corrected while the author was away from his own books, so that he was unable to make a final verification of two or three of the citations, but he trusts that they, as well as the others, are accurate. He takes this opportunity to acknowledge his indebtedness to Dr. Donald Blythe Durham, of Princeton University, for the preparation of the index.

Frank Frost Abbott. Einsiedeln, Switzerland *September 2, 1911*

## How Latin Became the Language of the World

How the armies of Rome mastered the nations of the world is known to every reader of history, but the story of the conquest by Latin of the languages of the world is vague in the minds of most of us. If we should ask ourselves how it came about, we should probably think of the world-wide supremacy of Latin as a natural result of the world-wide supremacy of the Roman legions or of Roman law. But in making this assumption we should be shutting our eyes to the history of our own times. A conquered people does not necessarily accept, perhaps it has not commonly accepted, the tongue of its master. In his "Ancient and Modern Imperialism" Lord Cromer states that in India only one hundred people in every ten thousand can read and write English, and this condition exists after an occupation of one hundred and fifty years or more. He adds: "There does not appear the least prospect of French supplanting Arabic in Algeria." In comparing the results of ancient and modern methods perhaps he should have taken into account the fact that India and Algeria have literatures of their own, which most of the outlying peoples subdued by Rome did not have, and these literatures may have strengthened the resistance which the tongue of the conquered people has offered to that of the conqueror, but, even when allowance is made for this fact, the difference in resultant conditions is surprising. From its narrow confines, within a little district on the banks of the Tiber, covering, at the close of the fifth century B.C., less than a hundred square miles, Latin spread through Italy and the islands of the Mediterranean, through France, Spain, England, northern Africa, and the Danubian provinces, triumphing over all the other tongues of those regions more completely than Roman arms triumphed over the peoples using them.

In tracing the story we must keep in our mind's eye the linguistic geography of Italy, just as we must remember the political geography of the peninsula in following Rome's territorial expansion. Let us think at the outset, then, of a little strip of flat country on the Tiber, dotted here and there with hills crowned with villages. Such hill towns were Rome, Tusculum, and Præneste, for instance. Each of them was the stronghold and market-place of the country immediately about it, and therefore had a life of its own, so that although Latin was spoken in all of them it varied from one to the other. This is shown clearly enough by the inscriptions which have been found on the sites of these ancient towns,[1] and as late as the close of the third century before our era, Plautus pokes fun in his comedies at the provincialism of Præneste.

The towns which we have mentioned were only a few miles from Rome. Beyond them, and occupying central Italy and a large part of southern Italy, were people who spoke Oscan and the other Italic dialects, which were related to Latin, and yet quite distinct from it. In the seaports of the south Greek was spoken, while the Messapians and Iapygians occupied Calabria. To the north of Rome were the mysterious Etruscans and the almost equally puzzling Venetians and Ligurians. When we follow the Roman legions across the Alps into Switzerland, France, England, Spain, and Africa, we enter a jungle, as it were, of languages and dialects. A mere reading of the list of tongues with which Latin was brought into contact, if such a list could be drawn up, would bring weariness to the flesh. In the part of Gaul conquered by Cæsar, for instance, he tells us that there were three independent languages, and sixty distinct states, whose peoples doubtless differed from one another in their speech. If we look at a map of the Roman world under Augustus, with the Atlantic to bound it on the west, the Euphrates on the east, the desert of Sahara on the south, and the Rhine and Danube on the north, and recall the fact that the linguistic conditions which Cæsar found in Gaul in 58 B.C. were typical of what confronted Latin in a great many of the western, southern, and northern provinces, the fact that Latin subdued all these different tongues, and became the every-day speech of these different peoples, will be recognized as one of the marvels of history. In fact, so firmly did it establish itself, that it withstood the assaults of the invading Gothic, Lombardic, Frankish, and Burgundian, and has continued to hold to our own day a very large part of the territory which it acquired some two thousand years ago.

That Latin was the common speech of the western world is attested not only by the fact that the languages of France, Spain, Roumania, and the other Romance countries descend from it, but it is also clearly shown by the thousands of Latin inscriptions composed by freeman and freedman, by carpenter, baker, and soldier, which we find all over the Roman world.

How did this extraordinary result come about? It was not the conquest of the world by the common language of Italy, because in Italy in early days at least nine different languages were spoken, but its subjugation by the tongue spoken in the city of Rome. The traditional narrative of Rome, as Livy and others relate it, tells us of a struggle with the neighboring Latin hill towns in the early days of the Republic, and the ultimate formation of an alliance between them and Rome. The favorable position of the city on the Tiber for trade and defence gave it a great advantage over its rivals, and it soon became the commercial and political centre of the neighboring territory. The most important of these villages, Tusculum, Præneste, and Lanuvium, were not more than twenty miles distant, and the people in them must have come constantly to Rome to attend the markets, and in later days to vote, to hear political speeches, and to listen to plays in the theatre. Some of them probably heard the jests at the expense of their dialectal peculiarities which Plautus introduced into his comedies. The younger generations became ashamed of their provincialisms; they imitated the Latin spoken in the metropolis, and by the second century of our era, when the Latin grammarians have occasion to cite dialectal peculiarities from Latium outside Rome, they quote at second-hand from Varro of the first century B.C., either because they will not take the trouble to use their own ears or because the differences which were noted in earlier days had ceased to exist. The first stage in the conquest of the world by the Latin of Rome comes to an end, then, with the extension of that form of speech throughout Latium.

Beyond the limits of Latium it came into contact with Oscan and the other Italic dialects, which were related to Latin, but of course were much farther removed from it than the Latin of Tusculum or Lanuvium had been,[2] so that the adoption of Latin was not so simple a matter as the acceptance of Roman Latin by the villages of Latium near Rome had been.

The conflict which went on between Latin and its Italic kinsmen is revealed to us now and then by a Latin inscription, into which Oscan or Umbrian forms have crept.[3] The struggle had come to an end by the beginning of our era. A few Oscan inscriptions are found scratched on the walls of Pompeii after the first earthquake, in 63 A.D., but they are late survivals, and no Umbrian inscriptions are known of a date subsequent to the first century B.C.

The Social War of 90-88 B.C., between Rome and the Italians, was a turning-point in the struggle between Latin and the Italic dialects, because it marks a change in the political treatment of Rome's dependencies in Italy. Up to this time she had followed the policy of isolating all her Italian conquered communities from one another.

She was anxious to prevent them from conspiring against her. Thus, with this object in view, she made differences in the rights and privileges granted to neighboring communities, in order that, not being subject to the same limitations, and therefore not having the same grievances, they might not have a common basis for joint action against her. It would naturally be a part of that policy to allow or to encourage the retention by the several communities of their own dialects. The common use of Latin would have enabled them to combine against her with greater ease. With the conclusion of the Social War this policy gave way before the new conception of political unity for the people of Italian stock, and with political unity came the introduction of Latin as the common tongue in all official transactions of a local as well as of a federal character. The immediate results of the war, and the policy which Rome carried out at its close of sending out colonies and building roads in Italy, contributed still more to the larger use of Latin throughout the central and southern parts of the peninsula. Samnium, Lucania, and the territory of the Bruttii suffered severely from depopulation; many colonies were sent into all these districts, so that, although the old dialects must have persisted for a time in some of the mountain towns to the north of Rome, the years following the conclusion of the Social War mark the rapid disappearance of them and the substitution of Latin in their place. Campania took little part in the war, and was therefore left untouched. This fact accounts probably for the occurrence of a few Oscan inscriptions on the walls of Pompeii as late as 63 A.D.

We need not follow here the story of the subjugation of the Greek seaports in southern Italy and of the peoples to the north who spoke non-Italic languages. In all these cases Latin was brought into conflict with languages not related to itself, and the situation contains slightly different elements from those which present themselves in the struggle between Latin and the Italic dialects. The latter were nearly enough related to Latin to furnish some support for the theory that Latin was modified by contact with them, and this theory has found advocates,[4] but there is no sufficient reason for believing that it was materially influenced. An interesting illustration of the influence of Greek on the Latin of every-day life is furnished by the realistic novel which Petronius wrote in the middle of the first century of our era. The characters in his story are Greeks, and the language which they speak is Latin, but they introduce into it a great many Greek words, and now and then a Greek idiom or construction.

The Romans, as is well known, used two agencies with great effect in Romanizing their newly acquired territory, viz., colonies and roads. The policy of sending out colonists to hold the new districts was definitely entered upon in the early part of the fourth century, when citizens were sent to Antium, Tarracina, and other points in Latium. Within this century fifteen or twenty colonies were established at various points in central Italy. Strategic considerations determined their location, and the choice was made with great wisdom. Sutrium and Nepete, on the borders of the Ciminian forest, were "the gates of Etruria"; Fregellæ and Interamna commanded the passage of the river Liris; Tarentum and Rhegium were important ports of entry, while Alba Fucens and Carsioli guarded the line of the Valerian road.

This road and the other great highways which were constructed in Italy brought not only all the colonies, but all parts of the peninsula, into easy communication with the capital. The earliest of them was built to Capua, as we know, by the great censor Appius Claudius, in 312 B.C., and when one looks at a map of Italy at the close of the third century before our era, and sees the central and southern parts of the peninsula dotted with colonies, the Appian Way running from Rome south-east to Brundisium, the Popillian Way to Rhegium, the Flaminian Way north-east to Ariminum, with an extension to Cremona, with the Cassian and Aurelian ways along the western coast, the rapidity and the completeness with which the Latin language overspread Italy ceases to be a mystery. A map of Spain or of France under the Empire, with its network of roads, is equally illuminating.

The missionaries who carried Roman law, Roman dress, Roman ideas, and the Latin language first through central, southern, and northern Italy, and then to the East and the West, were the colonist, the merchant, the soldier, and the federal official. The central government exempted the Roman citizen who settled in a provincial town from the local taxes. As these were very heavy, his advantage over the native was correspondingly great, and in almost all the large towns in the Empire we find evidence of the existence of large guilds of Roman traders, tax-collectors, bankers, and land-owners.[5] When Trajan in his romantic eastern campaign had penetrated to Ctesiphon, the capital of Parthia, he found Roman merchants already settled there. Besides the merchants and capitalists who were engaged in business on their own account in the provinces, there were thousands of agents for the great Roman corporations scattered through the Empire. Rome was the money centre of the world, and the great stock companies organized to lend money, construct public works, collect taxes, and engage in the shipping trade had their central offices in the capital whence they sent out their representatives to all parts of the world.

The soldier played as important a part as the merchant in extending the use of Latin. Tacitus tells us that in the reign of Augustus there were twenty-five legions stationed in the provinces. If we allow 6,000 men to a legion, we should have a total of 150,000 Roman soldiers scattered through the provinces. To these must be added the auxiliary troops which were made up of natives who, at the close of their term of service, were probably able to speak Latin, and when they settled among their own people again, would carry a knowledge of it into ever-widening circles. We have no exact knowledge of the number of the auxiliary troops, but they probably came to be as numerous as the legionaries.[6] Soldiers stationed on the frontiers frequently married native women at the end of their term of service, passed the rest of their lives in the provinces, and their children learned Latin.

The direct influence of the government was no small factor in developing the use of Latin, which was of course the official language of the Empire. All court proceedings were carried on in Latin. It was the language of the governor, the petty official, and the tax-gatherer. It was used in laws and proclamations, and no native could aspire to a post in the civil service unless he had mastered it. It was regarded sometimes at least as a *sine qua non* of the much-coveted Roman citizenship. The Emperor Claudius, for instance, cancelled the Roman citizenship of a Greek, because he had addressed a letter to him in Latin which he could not understand. The tradition that Latin was the official language of the world was taken up by the Christian church. Even when Constantine presided over the Council at Nicæa in the East, he addressed the assembly in Latin.

The two last-mentioned agencies, the Latin of the Roman official and the Latin of the church, were the influences which made the language spoken throughout the Empire essentially uniform in its character. Had the Latin which the colonist, the merchant, and the soldier carried through Italy and into the provinces been allowed to develop in different localities without any external unifying influence, probably new dialects would have grown up all over the world, or, to put it in another way, probably the Romance languages would have come into existence several centuries before they actually appeared. That unifying influence was the Latin used by the officials sent out from Rome, which all classes eagerly strove to imitate. Naturally the language of the provinces did not conform in all respects to the Roman standard. Apuleius, for instance, is aware of the fact that his African style and diction are likely to offend his Roman readers, and in the introduction to his *Metamorphoses* he begs for their indulgence. The elder Seneca in his *Controversiae* remarks of a Spanish fellow-countryman "that he could never unlearn that well-known style which is brusque and rustic and characteristic of Spain," and Spartianus in his Life of Hadrian tells us that when Hadrian addressed the senate on a certain occasion, his rustic pronunciation excited the laughter of the senators. But the peculiarities in the diction of Apuleius and Hadrian seem to have been those which only a cultivated man of the world would notice. They do not appear to have been fundamental. In a similar way the careful studies which have been made of the thousands of inscriptions found in the West[7], dedicatory inscriptions, guild records, and epitaphs show us that the language of the common people in the provinces did not differ materially from that spoken in Italy. It was the language of the Roman soldier, colonist, and trader, with common characteristics in the way of diction, form, phraseology, and syntax, dropping into some slight local peculiarities, but kept essentially a unit by the desire which each community felt to imitate its officials and its upper classes.

The one part of the Roman world in which Latin did not gain an undisputed pre-eminence was the Greek East. The Romans freely recognized the peculiar position which Greek was destined to hold in that part of the Empire, and styled it the *altera lingua*. Even in Greek lands, however, Latin gained a strong hold, and exerted considerable influence on Greek[8].

In a very thoughtful paper on "Language-Rivalry and Speech-Differentiation in the Case of Race-Mixture,"[9] Professor Hempl has discussed the conditions under which language-rivalry takes place, and states the results that follow. His conclusions have an interesting bearing on the question which we are discussing here, how and why it was that Latin supplanted the other languages with which it was brought into contact.

He observes that when two languages are brought into conflict, there is rarely a compromise or fusion, but one of the two is driven out of the field altogether by the other. On analyzing the circumstances in which such a struggle for supremacy between languages springs up, he finds four characteristic cases. Sometimes the armies of one nation, though comparatively small in numbers, conquer another country. They seize the government of the conquered land; their ruler becomes its king, and they become the aristocracy. They constitute a minority, however; they identify their interests with those of the conquered people, and the language of the subject people becomes the language of all classes. The second case arises when a country is conquered by a foreign people who pour into it with their wives and children through a long period and settle permanently there. The speech of the natives in these circumstances disappears. In the third case a more powerful people conquers a country, establishes a dependent government in it, sends out merchants, colonists, and officials, and establishes new towns. If such a province is held long enough, the language of the conqueror prevails. In the fourth and last case peaceful bands of immigrants enter a country to follow the humbler callings. They are scattered among the natives, and succeed in proportion as they learn the language of their adopted country. For their children and grandchildren this language becomes their mother tongue, and the speech of the invaded nation holds its ground.

The first typical case is illustrated by the history of Norman-French in England, the second by that of the European colonists in America; the Latinization of Spain, Gaul, and other Roman provinces furnishes an instance of the third, and our own experience with European immigrants is a case of the fourth characteristic situation. The third typical case of language-conflict is the one with which we are concerned here, and the analysis which we have made of the practices followed by the Romans in occupying newly acquired territory, both in Italy and outside the peninsula, shows us how closely they conform to the typical situation. With the exception of Dacia, all the provinces were held by the Romans for several centuries, so that their history under Roman rule satisfies the condition of long occupation which Professor Hempl lays down as a necessary one. Dacia which lay north of the Danube, and was thus far removed from the centres of Roman influence, was erected into a province in 107 A.D., and abandoned in 270. Notwithstanding its remoteness and the comparatively short period during which it was occupied, the Latin language has continued in use in that region to the present day. It furnishes therefore a striking illustration of the effective methods which the Romans used in Latinizing conquered territory.[10]

We have already had occasion to notice that a fusion between Latin and the languages with which it was brought into contact, such a fusion, for instance, as we find in Pidgin-English, did not occur. These languages influenced Latin only by way of making additions to its vocabulary. A great many Greek scientific and technical terms were adopted by the learned during the period of Roman supremacy. Of this one is clearly aware, for instance, in reading the philosophical and rhetorical works of Cicero. A few words, like rufus, crept into the language from the Italic dialects. Now and then the Keltic or Iberian names of Gallic or Spanish articles were taken up, but the inflectional system and the syntax of Latin retained their integrity. In the post-Roman period additions to the vocabulary are more significant. It is said that about three hundred Germanic words have found their way into all the Romance languages.[11] The language of the province of Gaul was most affected since some four hundred and fifty Gothic, Lombardic, and Burgundian words are found in French alone, such words as boulevard, homard, and blesser. Each of the provinces of course, when the Empire broke up, was subjected to influences peculiar to itself. The residence of the Moors in Spain, for seven hundred years, for instance, has left a deep impress on the Spanish vocabulary, while the geographic position of Roumanian has exposed it to the influence of Slavic, Albanian, Greek, Magyar, and Turkish.[12] A sketch of the history of Latin after the breaking up of the Empire carries us beyond the limits of the question which we set ourselves at the beginning and out of the domain of the Latinist, but it may not be out of place to gather together here a few of the facts which the Romance philologist has contributed to its later history, because the life of Latin has been continuous from the foundation of the city of Rome to the present day.

In this later period the question of paramount interest is, why did Latin in one part of the world develop into French, in another part into Italian, in another into Spanish? One answer to this question has been based on chronological grounds.[13] The Roman soldiers and traders who went out to garrison and to settle in a newly acquired territory, introduced that form of Latin which was in use in Italy at the time of their departure from the peninsula. The form of speech thus planted there developed along lines peculiar to itself, became the dialect of that province, and ultimately the (Romance) language spoken in that part of Europe. Sardinia was conquered in 241 B.C., and Sardinian therefore is a development of the Latin spoken in Italy in the middle of the third century B.C., that is of the Latin of Livius Andronicus. Spain was brought under Roman rule in 197 B.C., and consequently Spanish is a natural outgrowth of popular Latin of the time of Plautus. In a similar way, by noticing the date at which the several provinces were established down to the acquisition of Dacia in 107 A.D., we shall understand how it was that the several Romance languages developed out of Latin. So long as the Empire held together the unifying influence of official Latin, and the constant intercommunication between the provinces, preserved the essential unity of Latin throughout the world, but when the bonds were broken, the naturally divergent tendencies which had existed from the beginning, but had been held in check, made themselves felt, and the speech of the several sections of the Old World developed into the languages which we find in them to-day.

This theory is suggestive, and leads to several important results, but it is open to serious criticism, and does not furnish a sufficient explanation. It does not seem to take into account the steady stream of emigrants from Italy to the provinces, and the constant transfer of troops from one part of the world to another of which we become aware when we study the history of any single province or legion. Spain was acquired, it is true, in 197 B.C., and the Latin which was first introduced into it was the Latin of Plautus, but the subjugation of the country occupied more than sixty years, and during this period fresh troops were steadily poured into the peninsula, and later on there was frequently an interchange of legions between Spain and the other provinces. Furthermore, new communities of Roman citizens were established there even down into the Empire, and traders were steadily moving into the province. In this way it would seem that the Latin of the early second century which was originally carried into Spain must have been constantly undergoing modification, and, so far as this influence goes, made approximately like the Latin spoken elsewhere in the Empire.

A more satisfactory explanation seems to be that first clearly propounded by the Italian philologist, Ascoli. His reasoning is that when we acquire a foreign language we find it very difficult, and often impossible, to master some of the new sounds. Our ears do not catch them exactly, or we unconsciously substitute for the foreign sound some sound from our own language. Our vocal organs, too, do not adapt themselves readily to the reproduction of the strange sounds in another tongue, as we know from the difficulty which we have in pronouncing the French nasal or the German guttural. Similarly English differs somewhat as it is spoken by a Frenchman, a German, and an Italian. The Frenchman has a tendency to import the nasal into it, and he is also inclined to pronounce it like his own language, while the German favors the guttural. In a paper on the teaching of modern languages in our schools, Professor Grandgent says:[14] "Usually there is no attempt made to teach any French sounds but *u* and the four nasal vowels; all the rest are unquestioningly replaced by the English vowels and consonants that most nearly resemble them." The substitution of sounds from one's own language in speaking a foreign tongue, and the changes in voice-inflection, are more numerous and more marked if the man who learns the new language is uneducated and acquires it in casual intercourse from an uneducated man who speaks carelessly.

This was the state of things in the Roman provinces of southern Europe when the Goths, Lombards, and other peoples from the North gradually crossed the frontier and settled in the territory of Latin-speaking peoples. In the sixth century, for instance, the Lombards in Italy, the Franks in France, and the Visigoths in Spain would each give to the Latin which they spoke a twist peculiar to themselves, and out of the one Latin came Italian, out of the second, the language of France, and out of the third, Spanish. This initial impulse toward the development of Latin along different lines in Italy, France, and Spain was, of course, reinforced by differences in climate, in the temperaments of the three peoples, in their modes of life, and in their political and social experiences. These centrifugal forces, so to speak, became effective because the political and social bonds which had held Italy, France, and Spain together were now loosened, and consequently communication between the provinces was less frequent, and the standardizing influence of the official Latin of Rome ceased to keep Latin a uniform thing throughout the Empire.

One naturally asks why Latin survived at all, why the languages of the victorious Germanic peoples gave way to it. In reply to this question it is commonly said that the fittest survived, that the superiority of Roman civilization and of the Latin language gave Latin the victory. So far as this factor is to be taken into account, I should prefer to say that it was not so much the superiority of Latin, although that may be freely recognized, as it was the sentimental respect which the Germans and their leaders had for the Empire and for all its institutions. This is shown clearly enough, for instance, in the pride which the Visigothic and Frankish kings showed in holding their commissions from Rome, long after Rome had lost the power to enforce its claims upon them; it is shown in their use of Latin as the language of the court and of the official world. Under the influence of this sentiment Germanic rulers and their peoples imitated the Romans, and, among other things, took over their language. The church probably exerted considerable influence in this direction. Many of the Germans had been converted to Christianity before they entered the Empire, and had heard Latin used in the church services and in the hymns. Among cultivated people of different countries, it was the only medium of communication, and was accepted as the lingua franca of the political and ecclesiastical world, and the traditional medium of expression for literary and legal purposes.

Perhaps, however, one element in the situation should be given more weight than any of the facts just mentioned. Many of the barbarians had been allowed to settle in a more or less peaceful fashion in Roman territory, so that a large part of the western world came into their possession by way of gradual occupation rather than by conquest.[15] They became peasant proprietors, manual laborers, and soldiers in the Roman army. Perhaps, therefore, their occupation of central and southern Europe bears some resemblance to the peaceful invasion of this country by immigrants from Europe, and they may have adopted Latin just as the German or Scandinavian adopts English.

This brings us to the last important point in our inquiry. What is the date before which we shall call the language of the Western Empire Latin, and after which it is better to speak of French, Spanish, and Italian? Such a line of division cannot be sharply drawn, and will in a measure be artificial, because, as we shall attempt to show in the chapter which follows on the "Latin of the Common People," Latin survives in the Romance languages, and has had a continuous life up to the present day. But on practical grounds it is convenient to have such a line of demarcation in mind, and two attempts have been made to fix it. One attempt has been based on linguistic grounds, the other follows political changes more closely. Up to 700 A.D. certain common sound-changes take place in all parts of the western world.[16] After that date, roughly speaking, this is not the case. Consequently at that time we may say that unity ceased. The other method of approaching the subject leads to essentially the same conclusion, and shows us why unity ceased to exist.[17] In the sixth century the Eastern Emperor Justinian conceived the idea of reuniting the Roman world, and actually recovered and held for a short time Italy, southern Spain, and Africa. This attempt on his part aroused a national spirit among the peoples of these lands, and developed in them a sense of their national independence and individuality. They threw off the foreign yoke and became separate peoples, and developed, each of them, a language of its own. Naturally this sentiment became effective at somewhat different periods in different countries. For France the point may be fixed in the sixth century, for Spain and Italy, in the seventh, and at these dates Latin may be said to take the form of French, Spanish, and Italian.

## The Latin of the Common People

Unless one is a professional philologist he feels little interest in the language of the common people. Its peculiarities in pronunciation, syntax, phraseology, and the use of words we are inclined to avoid in our own speech, because they mark a lack of cultivation. We test them by the standards of polite society, and ignore them, or condemn them, or laugh at them as abnormal or illogical or indicative of ignorance. So far as literature goes, the speech of the common people has little interest for us because it is not the recognized literary medium. These two reasons have prevented the average man of cultivated tastes from giving much attention to the way in which the masses speak, and only the professional student has occupied himself with their language. This is unfortunate because the speech of the common people has many points of interest, and, instead of being illogical, is usually much more rigid in its adherence to its own accepted principles than formal speech is, which is likely to be influenced by convention or conventional associations. To take an illustration of what I have in mind, the ending *-s* is the common mark in English of a plural form. For instance, "caps," "maps," "lines," and "places" are plurals, and the corresponding singular forms are "cap," "map," "line," and "place." Consequently, granted the underlying premise, it is a perfectly logical and eminently scientific process from the forms "relapse" (pronounced, of course, "relaps") and "species" to postulate a corresponding singular, and speak of "a relap" and "a specie," as a negro of my acquaintance regularly does. "Scrope" and "lept," as preterites of "scrape" and "leap," are correctly formed on the analogy of "broke" and "crept," but are not used in polite society.

So far as English, German, or French go, a certain degree of general interest has been stimulated lately in the form which they take in every-day life by two very different agencies, by the popular articles of students of language, and by realistic and dialect novels. But for our knowledge of the Latin of the common people we lack these two all-important sources of information. It occurred to only two Roman writers, Petronius and Apuleius, to amuse their countrymen by writing realistic stories, or stories with realistic features, and the Roman grammarian felt an even greater contempt for popular Latin or a greater indifference to it than we feel to-day. This feeling was shared, as we know, by the great humanists of the fourteenth and fifteenth centuries, when the revival of interest in the Greek and Latin languages and literatures begins. Petrarch, Poggio Bracciolini, and the other great leaders in the movement were concerned with the literary aspects of the classics, and the scholars of succeeding generations, so far as they studied the language, confined their attention to that of the great Latin stylists. The first student to conceive of the existence of popular Latin as a form of speech which differed from formal literary Latin, seems to have been the French scholar, Henri Étienne. In a little pamphlet on the language and style of Plautus, written toward the end of the sixteenth century, he noted the likeness between French and the language of the Latin dramatist, without, however, clearly perceiving that the reason for this similarity lay in the fact that the comedies of Plautus reflect the spoken language of his time, and that French and the other Romance languages have developed out of this, rather than from literary Latin. Not until the middle of the eighteenth century was this truth clearly recognized, and then almost simultaneously on both sides of the Rhine.

It was left for the nineteenth century, however, to furnish scientific proof of the correctness of this hypothesis, and it was a fitting thing that the existence of an unbroken line of connection between popular Latin of the third century before our era, and the Romance languages of the nineteenth century, should have been established at the same time by a Latinist engaged in the study of Plautus, and a Romance philologist working upward toward Latin. The Latin scholar was Ritschl, who showed that the deviations from the formal standard which one finds in Plautus are not anomalies or mistakes, but specimens of colloquial Latin which can be traced down into the later period. The Romance philologist was Diez, who found that certain forms and words, especially those from the vocabulary of every-day life, which are common to many of the Romance languages, are not to be found in serious Latin literature at all, but occur only in those compositions, like comedy, satire, or the realistic romance, which reflect the speech of the every-day man. This discovery made it clear that the Romance languages are related to folk Latin, not to literary Latin. It is sixty years since the study of vulgar Latin was put on a scientific basis by the investigations of these two men, and during that period the Latinist and the Romance philologist have joined hands in extending our knowledge of it. From the Latin side a great impetus was given to the work by the foundation in 1884 of Wölfflin's *Archiv für lateinische Lexikographie und Grammatik*. This periodical, as is well known, was intended to prepare the way for the publication of the Latin *Thesaurus*, which the five German Academies are now bringing out.

One of its primary purposes, as its title indicates, was to investigate the history of Latin words, and in its first number the editor called attention to the importance of knowing the pieces of literature in which each Latin word or locution occurred. The results have been very illuminating. Some words or constructions or phrases are to be found, for instance, only in comedy, satire, and the romance. They are evidently peculiar to vulgar Latin. Others are freely used in these types of literature, but sparingly employed in historical or rhetorical works. Here again a shade of difference is noticeable between formal and familiar usage. The method of the Latinist then is essentially one of comparison and contrast. When, for instance, he finds the word *equus* regularly used by serious writers for "horse," but *caballus* employed in that sense in the colloquial compositions of Lucilius, Horace, and Petronius, he comes to the conclusion that *caballus* belongs to the vocabulary of every-day life, that it is our "nag."

The line of reasoning which the Romance philologist follows in his study of vulgar Latin is equally convincing. The existence of a large number of words and idioms in French, Spanish, Italian, and the other Romance languages can be explained only in one of three ways. All these different languages may have hit on the same word or phrase to express an idea, or these words and idioms may have been borrowed from one language by the others, or they may come from a common origin. The first hypothesis is unthinkable. The second is almost as impossible. Undoubtedly French, for instance, borrowed some words from Spanish, and Spanish from Portuguese. It would be conceivable that a few words originating in Spain should pass into France, and thence into Italy, but it is quite beyond belief that the large element which the languages from Spain to Roumania have in common should have passed by borrowing over such a wide territory. It is clear that this common element is inherited from Latin, out of which all the Romance languages are derived. Out of the words, endings, idioms, and constructions which French, Spanish, Italian, and the other tongues of southern Europe have in common, it would be possible, within certain limits, to reconstruct the parent speech, but fortunately we are not limited to this material alone. At this point the Latinist and the Romance philologist join hands. To take up again the illustration already used, the student of the Romance languages finds the word for "horse" in Italian is cavallo, in Spanish caballo, in French cheval, in Roumanian cal, and so on. Evidently all these forms have come from caballus, which the Latinist finds belongs to the vocabulary of vulgar, not of formal,

Latin. This one illustration out of many not only discloses the fact that the Romance languages are to be connected with colloquial rather than with literary Latin, but it also shows how the line of investigation opened by Diez, and that followed by Wölfflin and his school, supplement each other. By the use of the methods which these two scholars introduced, a large amount of material bearing on the subject under discussion has been collected and classified, and the characteristic features of the Latin of the common people have been determined. It has been found that five or six different and independent kinds of evidence may be used in reconstructing this form of speech.

We naturally think first of the direct statements made by Latin writers. These are to be found in the writings of Cicero, Quintilian, Seneca the Rhetorician, Petronius, Aulus Gellius, Vitruvius, and the Latin grammarians. The professional teacher Quintilian is shocked at the illiterate speech of the spectators in the theatres and circus. Similarly a character in Petronius utters a warning against the words such people use. Cicero openly delights in using every-day Latin in his familiar letters, while the architect Vitruvius expresses the anxious fear that he may not be following the accepted rules of grammar. As we have noticed above, a great deal of material showing the differences between formal and colloquial Latin which these writers have in mind, may be obtained by comparing, for instance, the Letters of Cicero with his rhetorical works, or Seneca's satirical skit on the Emperor Claudius with his philosophical writings. Now and then, too, a serious writer has occasion to use a bit of popular Latin, but he conveniently labels it for us with an apologetic phrase. Thus even St. Jerome, in his commentary on the Epistle to the Ephesians, says: "Don't look a gift horse in the mouth, as the vulgar proverb has it." To the ancient grammarians the "mistakes" and vulgarisms of popular speech were abhorrent, and they have fortunately branded lists of words and expressions which are not to be used by cultivated people. The evidence which may be had from the Romance languages, supplemented by Latin, not only contributes to our knowledge of the vocabulary of vulgar Latin, but it also shows us many common idioms and constructions which that form of speech had. Thus, "I will sing" in Italian is canterò (=cantar[e]-ho), in Spanish, cantaré (=cantar-he), in French, chanterai (=chanter-ai), and similar forms occur in some of the other Romance languages. These forms are evidently made up of the Latin infinitive cantare, depending on habeo ("I have to sing"). But the future in literary Latin was cantabo, formed by adding an ending, as we know, and with that the Romance future can have no connection. However, as a writer in the *Archiv* has pointed out,[18] just such analytical tense forms as are used in the Romance languages to-day are to be found in the popular Latin sermons of St. Jerome. From these idioms, common to Italian, French, and Spanish, then, we can reconstruct a Latin formation current among the common people. Finally a knowledge of the tendencies and practices of spoken English helps us to identify similar usages when we come upon them in our reading of Latin. When, for instance, the slave in a play of Plautus says: "Do you catch on" (tenes?), "I'll touch the old man for a loan" (tangam senem, etc.), or "I put it over him" (ei os sublevi) we recognize specimens of Latin slang, because all of the metaphors involved are in current use to-day. When one of the freedmen in Petronius remarks: "You ought not to do a good turn to nobody" (neminem nihil boni facere oportet) we see the same use of the double negative to which we are accustomed in illiterate English. The rapid survey which we have just made of the evidence bearing on the subject establishes beyond doubt the existence of a form of speech among the Romans which cannot be identified with literary Latin, but it has been held by some writers that the material for the study of it is scanty. However, an impartial examination of the facts ought not to lead one to this conclusion. On the Latin side the material includes the comedies of Plautus and Terence, and the comic fragments, the familiar odes of Catullus, the satires of Lucilius, Horace, and Seneca, and here and there of Persius and Juvenal, the familiar letters of Cicero, the romance of Petronius and that of Apuleius in part, the Vulgate and some of the Christian fathers, the Journey to Jerusalem of St. Ætheria, the glossaries, some technical books like Vitruvius and the veterinary treatise of Chiron, and the private inscriptions, notably epitaphs, the wall inscriptions of Pompeii, and the leaden tablets found buried in the ground on which illiterate people wrote curses upon their enemies.

It is clear that there has been preserved for the study of colloquial Latin a very large body of material, coming from a great variety of sources and running in point of time from Plautus in the third century B.C. to St. Ætheria in the latter part of the fourth century or later. It includes books by trained writers, like Horace and Petronius, who consciously adopt the Latin of every-day life, and productions by uneducated people, like St. Ætheria and the writers of epitaphs, who have unwittingly used it.

St. Jerome says somewhere of spoken Latin that "it changes constantly as you pass from one district to another, and from one period to another" (et ipsa Latinitas et regionibus cotidie mutatur et tempore). If he had added that it varies with circumstances also, he would have included the three factors which have most to do in influencing the development of any spoken language. We are made aware of the changes which time has brought about in colloquial English when we compare the conversations in Fielding with those in a present-day novel. When a spoken language is judged by the standard of the corresponding literary medium, in some of its aspects it proves to be conservative, in others progressive. It shows its conservative tendency by retaining many words and phrases which have passed out of literary use. The English of the Biglow Papers, when compared with the literary speech of the time, abundantly illustrates this fact. This conservative tendency is especially noticeable in districts remote from literary centres, and those of us who are familiar with the vernacular in Vermont or Maine will recall in it many quaint words and expressions which literature abandoned long ago. In Virginia locutions may be heard which have scarcely been current in literature since Shakespeare's time. Now, literary and colloquial Latin were probably drawn farther apart than the two corresponding forms of speech in English, because Latin writers tried to make the literary tongue as much like Greek in its form as possible, so that literary Latin would naturally have diverged more rapidly and more widely from conversational Latin than formal English has drawn away from colloquial English.

But a spoken language in its development is progressive as well as conservative. To certain modifying influences it is especially sensitive. It is fond of the concrete, picturesque, and novel, and has a high appreciation of humor. These tendencies lead it to invent many new words and expressions which must wait months, years, perhaps a generation, before they are accepted in literature. Sometimes they are never accepted. The history of such words as buncombe, dude, Mugwump, gerrymander, and joy-ride illustrate for English the fact that words of a certain kind meet a more hospitable reception in the spoken language than they do in literature. The writer of comedy or farce, the humorist, and the man in the street do not feel the constraint which the canons of good usage put on the serious writer. They coin new words or use old words in a new way or use new constructions without much hesitation. The extraordinary material progress of the modern world during the last century has undoubtedly stimulated this tendency in a remarkable way, but it would seem as if the Latin of the common people from the time of Plautus to that of Cicero must have been subjected to still more innovating influences than modern conversational English has. During this period the newly conquered territories in Spain, northern Africa, Greece, and Asia poured their slaves and traders into Italy, and added a great many words to the vocabulary of every-day life. The large admixture of Greek words and idioms in the language of Petronius in the first century of our era furnishes proof of this fact. A still greater influence must have been felt within the language itself by the stimulus to the imagination which the coming of these foreigners brought, with their new ideas, and their new ways of looking at things, their strange costumes, manners, and religions.

The second important factor which affects the spoken language is a difference in culture and training. The speech of the gentleman differs from that of the rustic. The conversational language of Terence, for instance, is on a higher plane than that of Plautus, while the characters in Plautus use better Latin than the freedmen in Petronius. The illiterate freedmen in Petronius speak very differently from the freemen in his story. Sometimes a particular occupation materially affects the speech of those who pursue it. All of us know something of the linguistic eccentricities of the London cabman, the Parisian thief, or the American hobo. This particular influence cannot be estimated so well for Latin because we lack sufficient material, but some progress has been made in detecting the peculiarities of Latin of the nursery, the camp, and the sea.

Of course a spoken language is never uniform throughout a given area. Dialectal differences are sure to develop. A man from Indiana and another from Maine will be sure to notice each other's peculiarities. Even the railway, the newspaper, and the public school will never entirely obliterate the old differences or prevent new ones from springing up. Without these agencies which do so much to promote uniformity to-day, Italy and the rest of the Empire must have shown greater dialectal differences than we observe in American English or in British English even.

For the sake of bringing out clearly some of the points of difference between vulgar and formal Latin we have used certain illustrations, like *caballus*, where the two forms of speech were radically opposed to each other, but of course they did not constitute two different languages, and that which they had in common was far greater than the element peculiar to each, or, to put it in another way, they in large measure overlapped each other. Perhaps we are in a position now to characterize colloquial Latin and to define it as the language which was used in conversation throughout the Empire with the innumerable variations which time and place gave it, which in its most highly refined form, as spoken in literary circles at Rome in the classical period, approached indefinitely near its ideal, literary Latin, which in its most unconventional phase was the rude speech of the rabble, or the "sermo inconditus" of the ancients. The facts which have just been mentioned may be illustrated by the accompanying diagrams.

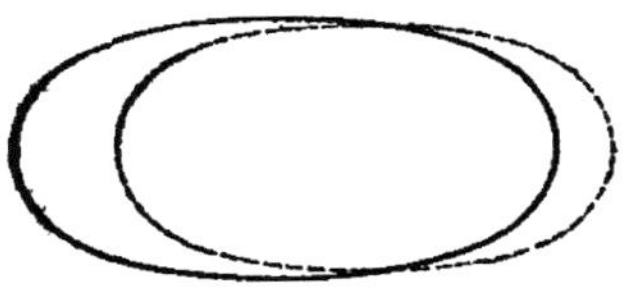

Fig I

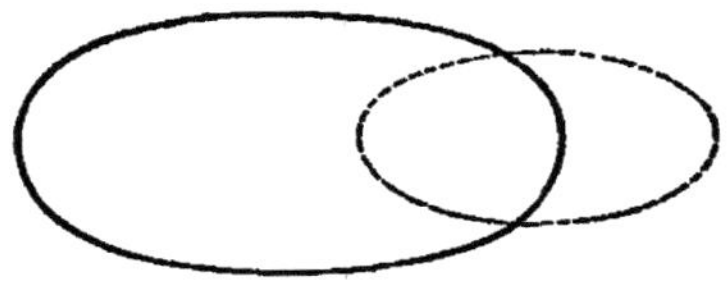

Fig.II

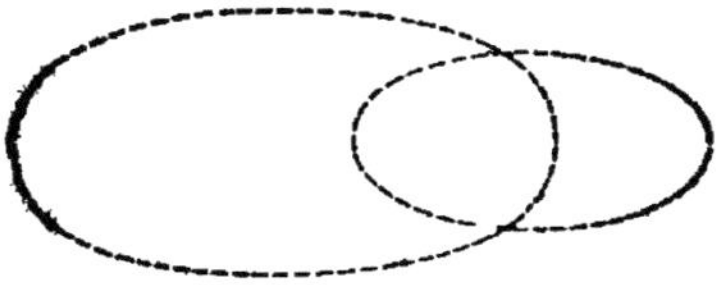

Fig III

Fig.IV

In Fig. I the heavy-lined ellipse represents the formal diction of Cicero, the dotted line ellipse his conversational vocabulary. They overlap each other through a great part of their extent, but there are certain literary locutions which would rarely be used by him in conversation, and certain colloquial words and phrases which he would not use in formal writing. Therefore the two ellipses would not be coterminous. In Fig. II the heavy ellipse has the same meaning as in Fig. I, while the space enclosed by the dotted line represents the vocabulary of an uneducated Roman, which would be much smaller than that of Cicero and would show a greater degree of difference from the literary vocabulary than Cicero's conversational stock of words does. The relation of the uncultivated Roman's conversational vocabulary to that of Cicero is illustrated in Fig. III, while Fig. IV shows how the Latin of the average man in Rome would compare, for instance, with that of a resident of Lugudunum, in Gaul.

This naturally brings us to consider the historical relations of literary and colloquial Latin. In explaining them it has often been assumed that colloquial Latin is a degenerate form of literary Latin, or that the latter is a refined type of the former. Both these theories are equally false. Neither is derived from the other. The true state of the case has never been better put than by Schuchardt, who says: "Vulgar Latin stands with reference to formal Latin in no derivative relation, in no paternal relation, but they stand side by side. It is true that vulgar Latin came from a Latin with fuller and freer forms, but it did not come from formal Latin. It is true that formal Latin came from a Latin of a more popular and a cruder character, but it did not come from vulgar Latin. In the original speech of the people, preliterary Latin (the prisca Latinitas), is to be found the origin of both; they were twin brothers."

Of this preliterary Latin we have no record. The best we can do is to infer what its characteristics were from the earliest fragments of the language which have come down to us, from the laws of the Twelve Tables, for instance, from the religious and legal formulæ preserved to us by Varro, Cicero, Livy, and others, from proverbs and popular sayings. It would take us too far afield to analyze these documents here, but it may be observed that we notice in them, among other characteristics, an indifference to strict grammatical structure, not that subordination of clauses to a main clause which comes only from an appreciation of the logical relation of ideas to one another, but a co-ordination of clauses, the heaping up of synonymous words, a tendency to use the analytical rather than the synthetical form of expression, and a lack of fixity in the forms of words and in inflectional endings. To illustrate some of these traits in a single example, an early law reads "if [he] shall have committed a theft by night, if [he] shall have killed him, let him be regarded as put to death legally" (si nox furtum faxsit, si im occisit, iure caesus esto).[19] We pass without warning from one subject, the thief, in the first clause to another, the householder, in the second, and back to the thief again in the third. Cato in his book on Agriculture writes of the cattle: "let them feed; it will be better" (pascantur; satius erit), instead of saying: "it will be better for them to feed" (or "that they feed"). In an early law one reads: "on the tablet, on the white surface" (in tabula, in albo), instead of "on the white tablet" (in alba tabula). Perhaps we may sum up the general characteristics of this preliterary Latin out of which both the spoken and written language developed by saying that it showed a tendency to analysis rather than synthesis, a loose and variable grammatical structure, and a lack of logic in expression.

Livius Andronicus, Nævius, and Plautus in the third century before our era show the language as first used for literary purposes, and with them the breach between the spoken and written tongues begins. So far as Livius Andronicus, the Father of Latin literature, is concerned, allowance should be made without doubt for his lack of poetic inspiration and skill, and for the fact that his principal work was a translation, but even making this allowance the crude character of his Latin is apparent, and it is very clear that literary Latin underwent a complete transformation between his time and that of Horace and Virgil. Now, the significant thing in this connection is the fact that this transformation was largely brought about under an external influence, which affected the Latin of the common people only indirectly and in small measure. Perhaps the circumstances in which literary Latin was placed have never been repeated in history. At the very outset it was brought under the sway of a highly developed literary tongue, and all the writers who subsequently used it earnestly strove to model it after Greek. Livius Andronicus, Ennius, Accius, and Pacuvius were all of Greek origin and familiar with Greek. They, as well as Plautus and Terence, translated and adapted Greek epics, tragedies, and comedies. Several of the early writers, like Accius and Lucilius, interested themselves in grammatical subjects, and did their best to introduce system and regularity into their literary medium. Now, Greek was a highly inflected, synthetical, regular, and logical medium of literary expression, and it was inevitable that these qualities should be introduced into Latin. But this influence affected the spoken language very little, as we have already noticed. Its effect upon the speech of the common people would be slight, because of the absence of the common school which does so much to-day to hold together the spoken and written languages.

The development then of preliterary Latin under the influence of this systematizing, synthetical influence gave rise to literary Latin, while its independent growth more nearly in accordance with its original genius produced colloquial Latin. Consequently, we are not surprised to find that the people's speech retained in a larger measure than literary Latin did those qualities which we noticed in preliterary Latin. Those characteristics are, in fact, to be expected in conversation. When a man sets down his thoughts on paper he expresses himself with care and with a certain reserve in his statements, and he usually has in mind exactly what he wants to say. But in speaking he is not under this constraint. He is likely to express himself in a tautological, careless, or even illogical fashion. He rarely thinks out to the end what he has in mind, but loosely adds clauses or sentences, as new ideas occur to him.

We have just been thinking mainly about the relation of words to one another in a sentence. In the treatment of individual words, written and spoken Latin developed along different lines. In English we make little distinction between the quantity of vowels, but in Latin of course a given vowel was either long or short, and literary tradition became so fixed in this matter that the professional poets of the Augustan age do not tolerate any deviation from it. There are indications, however, that the common people did not observe the rules of quantity in their integrity. We can readily understand why that may have been the case. The comparative carelessness, which is characteristic of conversation, affects our pronunciation of words. When there is a stress accent, as there was in Latin, this is especially liable to be the case. We know in English how much the unaccented syllables suffer in a long word like "laboratory." In Latin the long unaccented vowels and the final syllable, which was never protected by the accent, were peculiarly likely to lose their full value. As a result, in conversational Latin certain final consonants tended to drop away, and probably the long vowel following a short one was regularly shortened when the accent fell on the short syllable, or on the syllable which followed the long one. Some scholars go so far as to maintain that in course of time all distinction in quantity in the unaccented vowels was lost in popular Latin. Sometimes the influence of the accent led to the excision of the vowel in the syllable which followed it. Probus, a grammarian of the fourth century of our era, in what we might call a "Guide to Good Usage"[20] or "One Hundred Words Mispronounced," warns his readers against masclus and anglus for masculus and angulus. This is the same popular tendency which we see illustrated in "lab'ratory."

The quality of vowels as well as their quantity changed. The obscuring of certain vowel sounds in ordinary or careless conversation in this country in such words as "Latun" and "Amurican" is a phenomenon which is familiar enough. In fact a large number of our vowel sounds seem to have degenerated into a grunt. Latin was affected in a somewhat similar way, although not to the same extent as present-day English. Both the ancient grammarians in their warnings and the Romance languages bear evidence to this effect.

We noticed above that the final consonant was exposed to danger by the fact that the syllable containing it was never protected by the accent. It is also true that there was a tendency to do away with any difficult combination of consonants. We recall in English the current pronunciations, "February," and "Calwell" for Caldwell. The average Roman in the same way was inclined to follow the line of least resistance. Sometimes, as in the two English examples just given, he avoided a difficult combination of consonants by dropping one of them. This method he followed in saying santus for sanctus, and scriserunt for scripserunt, just as in vulgar English one now and then hears "slep" and "kep" for the more difficult "slept" and "kept." Sometimes he lightened the pronunciation by metathesis, as he did when he pronounced interpretor as interpertor. A third device was to insert a vowel, as illiterate English-speaking people do in the pronunciations "ellum" and "Henery." In this way, for instance, the Roman avoided the difficult combinations -mn- and -chn- by saying mina and techina for the historically correct mna and techna. Another method of surmounting the difficulty was to assimilate one of the two consonants to the other. This is a favorite practice of the shop-girl, over which the newspapers make merry in their phonetical reproductions of supposed conversations heard from behind the counter. Adopting the same easy way of speaking, the uneducated Roman sometimes said isse for ipse, and scritus for scriptus. To pass to another point of difference, the laws determining the incidence of the accent were very firmly established in literary Latin. The accent must fall on the penult, if it was long, otherwise on the antepenult of the word. But in popular Latin there were certain classes of words in whose case these principles were not observed.

The very nature of the accent probably differed in the two forms of speech. In preliterary Latin the stress was undoubtedly a marked feature of the accent, and this continued to be the case in the popular speech throughout the entire history of the language, but, as I have tried to prove in another paper,[21] in formal Latin the stress became very slight, and the pitch grew to be the characteristic feature of the accent. Consequently, when Virgil read a passage of the *Æneid* to Augustus and Livia the effect on the ear of the comparatively unstressed language, with the rhythmical rise and fall of the pitch, would have been very different from that made by the conversation of the average man, with the accented syllables more clearly marked by a stress.

In this brief chapter we cannot attempt to go into details, and in speaking of the morphology of vulgar Latin we must content ourselves with sketching its general characteristics and tendencies, as we have done in the case of its phonology. In English our inflectional forms have been reduced to a minimum, and consequently there is little scope for differences in this respect between the written and spoken languages. From the analogy of other forms the illiterate man occasionally says: "I swum," or, "I clumb," or "he don't," but there is little chance of making a mistake. However, with three genders, five declensions for nouns, a fixed method of comparison for adjectives and adverbs, an elaborate system of pronouns, with active and deponent, regular and irregular verbs, four conjugations, and a complex synthetical method of forming the moods and tenses, the pitfalls for the unwary Roman were without number, as the present-day student of Latin can testify to his sorrow. That the man in the street, who had no newspaper to standardize his Latin, and little chance to learn it in school, did not make more mistakes is surprising. In a way many of the errors which he did make were historically not errors at all. This fact will readily appear from an illustration or two. In our survey of preliterary Latin we had occasion to notice that one of its characteristics was a lack of fixity in the use of forms or constructions. In the third century before our era, a Roman could say audibo or audiam, contemplor or contemplo, senatus consultum or senati consultum. Thanks to the efforts of the scientific grammarian, and to the systematizing influence which Greek exerted upon literary Latin, most verbs were made deponent or active once for all, a given noun was permanently assigned to a particular declension, a verb to one conjugation, and the slight tendency which the language had to the analytical method of forming the moods and tenses was summarily checked. Of course the common people tried to imitate their betters in all these matters, but the old variable usages persisted to some extent, and the average man failed to grasp the niceties of the new grammar at many points. His failures were especially noticeable where the accepted literary form did not seem to follow the principles of analogy. When these principles are involved, the common people are sticklers for consistency. The educated man conjugates: "I don't," "you don't," "he doesn't," "we don't," "they don't"; but the anomalous form "he doesn't" has to give way in the speech of the average man to "he don't." To take only one illustration in Latin of the effect of the same influence, the present infinitive active of almost all verbs ends in -re, e.g., amare, monere, and regere. Consequently the irregular infinitive of the verb "to be able," posse, could not stand its ground, and ultimately became potere in vulgar Latin. In one respect in the inflectional forms of the verb, the purist was unexpectedly successful. In comedy of the third and second centuries B.C., we find sporadic evidence of a tendency to use auxiliary verbs in forming certain tenses, as we do in English when we say: "I will go," "I have gone," or "I had gone." This movement was thoroughly stamped out for the time, and does not reappear until comparatively late.

In Latin there are three genders, and the grammatical gender of a noun is not necessarily identical with its natural gender. For inanimate objects it is often determined simply by the form of the noun. Sella, seat, of the first declension, is feminine, because almost all nouns ending in -a are feminine; hortus, garden, is masculine, because nouns in -us of its declension are mostly masculine, and so on. From such a system as this two results are reasonably sure to follow. Where the gender of a noun in literary Latin did not conform to these rules, in popular Latin it would be brought into harmony with others of its class. Thus stigma, one of the few neuter nouns in -a, and consequently assigned to the third declension, was brought in popular speech into line with sella and the long list of similar words in -a, was made feminine, and put in the first declension. In the case of another class of words, analogy was supplemented by a mechanical influence. We have noticed already that the tendency of the stressed syllable in a word to absorb effort and attention led to the obscuration of certain final consonants, because the final syllable was never protected by the accent. Thus hortus in some parts of the Empire became hortu in ordinary pronunciation, and the neuter caelum, heaven, became caelu. The consequent identity in the ending led to a confusion in the gender, and to the ultimate treatment of the word for "heaven" as a masculine. These influences and others caused many changes in the gender of nouns in popular speech, and in course of time brought about the elimination of the neuter gender from the neo-Latin languages.

Something has been said already of the vocabulary of the common people. It was naturally much smaller than that of cultivated people. Its poverty made their style monotonous when they had occasion to express themselves in writing, as one can see in reading St. Ætheria's account of her journey to the Holy Land, and of course this impression of monotony is heightened by such a writer's inability to vary the form of expression. Even within its small range it differs from the vocabulary of formal Latin in three or four important respects. It has no occasion, or little occasion, to use certain words which a formal writer employs, or it uses substitutes for them. So testa was used in part for caput, and bucca for os. On the other hand, it employs certain words and phrases, for instance vulgar words and expletives, which are not admitted into literature.

In its choice of words it shows a marked preference for certain suffixes and prefixes. It would furnish an interesting excursion into folk psychology to speculate on the reasons for this preference in one case and another. Sometimes it is possible to make out the influence at work. In reading a piece of popular Latin one is very likely to be impressed with the large number of diminutives which are used, sometimes in the strict sense of the primitive word. The frequency of this usage reminds one in turn of the fact that not infrequently in the Romance languages the corresponding words are diminutive forms in their origin, so that evidently the diminutive in these cases crowded out the primitive word in popular use, and has continued to our own day. The reason why the diminutive ending was favored does not seem far to seek. That suffix properly indicates that the object in question is smaller than the average of its kind. Smallness in a child stimulates our affection, in a dwarf, pity or aversion. Now we give expression to our emotion more readily in the intercourse of every-day life than we do in writing, and the emotions of the masses are perhaps nearer the surface and more readily stirred than are those of the classes, and many things excite them which would leave unruffled the feelings of those who are more conventional. The stirring of these emotions finds expression in the use of the diminutive ending, which indirectly, as we have seen, suggests sympathy, affection, pity, or contempt. The ending -osus for adjectives was favored because of its sonorous character. Certain prefixes, like de-, dis-, and ex-, were freely used with verbs, because they strengthened the meaning of the verb, and popular speech is inclined to emphasize its ideas unduly.

To speak further of derivation, in the matter of compounds and crystallized word groups there are usually differences between a spoken and written language. The written language is apt to establish certain canons which the people do not observe. For instance, we avoid hybrid compounds of Greek and Latin elements in the serious writing of English. In formal Latin we notice the same objection to Greco-Latin words, and yet in Plautus, and in other colloquial writers, such compounds are freely used for comic effect. In a somewhat similar category belong the combinations of two adverbs or prepositions, which one finds in the later popular Latin, some of which have survived in the Romance languages. A case in point is ab ante, which has come down to us in the Italian avanti and the French avant. Such word-groups are of course debarred from formal speech.

In examining the vocabulary of colloquial Latin, we have noticed its comparative poverty, its need of certain words which are not required in formal Latin, its preference for certain prefixes and suffixes, and its willingness to violate certain rules, in forming compounds and word-groups, which the written language scrupulously observes. It remains for us to consider a third, and perhaps the most important, element of difference between the vocabularies of the two forms of speech. I mean the use of a word in vulgar Latin with another meaning from that which it has in formal Latin. We are familiar enough with the different senses which a word often has in conversational and in literary English. "Funny," for instance, means "amusing" in formal English, but it is often the synonym of "strange" in conversation. The sense of a word may be extended, or be restricted, or there may be a transfer of meaning. In the colloquial use of "funny" we have an extension of its literary sense. The same is true of "splendid," "jolly," "lovely," and "awfully," and of such Latin words as "lepidus," "probe," and "pulchre." When we speak of "a splendid sun," we are using splendid in its proper sense of shining or bright, but when we say, "a splendid fellow," the adjective is used as a general epithet expressing admiration. On the other hand, when a man of a certain class refers to his "woman," he is employing the word in the restricted sense of "wife." Perhaps we should put in a third category that very large colloquial use of words in a transferred or figurative sense, which is illustrated by "to touch" or "to strike" when applied to success in getting money from a person. Our current slang is characterized by the free use of words in this figurative way.

Under the head of syntax we must content ourselves with speaking of only two changes, but these were far-reaching. We have already noticed the analytical tendency of preliterary Latin. This tendency was held in check, as we have just observed, so far as verb forms were concerned, but in the comparison of adjectives and in the use of the cases it steadily made headway, and ultimately triumphed over the synthetical principle. The method adopted by literary Latin of indicating the comparative and the superlative degrees of an adjective, by adding the endings -ior and -issimus respectively, succumbed in the end to the practice of prefixing plus or magis and maxime to the positive form. To take another illustration of the same characteristic of popular Latin, as early as the time of Plautus, we see a tendency to adopt our modern method of indicating the relation which a substantive bears to some other word in the sentence by means of a preposition rather than by simply using a case form. The careless Roman was inclined to say, for instance, magna pars de exercitu, rather than to use the genitive case of the word for army, magna pars exercitus. Perhaps it seemed to him to bring out the relation a little more clearly or forcibly.

The use of a preposition to show the relation became almost a necessity when certain final consonants became silent, because with their disappearance, and the reduction of the vowels to a uniform quantity, it was often difficult to distinguish between the cases. Since final -m was lost in pronunciation, *Asia* might be nominative, accusative, or ablative. If you wished to say that something happened in Asia, it would not suffice to use the simple ablative, because that form would have the same pronunciation as the nominative or the accusative, Asia(m), but the preposition must be prefixed, *in Asia*. Another factor cooperated with those which have already been mentioned in bringing about the confusion of the cases. Certain prepositions were used with the accusative to indicate one relation, and with the ablative to suggest another. *In Asia,* for instance, meant "in Asia," *in Asiam,* "into Asia." When the two case forms became identical in pronunciation, the meaning of the phrase would be determined by the verb in the sentence, so that with a verb of going the preposition would mean "into," while with a verb of rest it would mean "in." In other words the idea of motion or rest is disassociated from the case forms. From the analogy of *in* it was very easy to pass to other prepositions like *per,* which in literary Latin took the accusative only, and to use these prepositions also with cases which, historically speaking, were ablatives.

In his heart of hearts the school-boy regards the periodic sentences which Cicero hurled at Catiline, and which Livy used in telling the story of Rome as unnatural and perverse. All the specious arguments which his teacher urges upon him, to prove that the periodic form of expression was just as natural to the Roman as the direct method is to us, fail to convince him that he is not right in his feeling--and he *is* right. Of course in English, as a rule, the subject must precede the verb, the object must follow it, and the adverb and attribute adjective must stand before the words to which they belong. In the sentence: "Octavianus wished Cicero to be saved," not a single change may be made in the order without changing the sense, but in a language like Latin, where relations are largely expressed by inflectional forms, almost any order is possible, so that a writer may vary his arrangement and grouping of words to suit the thought which he wishes to convey. But this is a different matter from the construction of a period with its main subject at the beginning, its main verb at the end, and all sorts of subordinate and modifying clauses locked in by these two words. This was not the way in which the Romans talked with one another. We can see that plainly enough from the conversations in Plautus and Terence. In fact the Latin period is an artificial product, brought to perfection by many generations of literary workers, and the nearer we get to the Latin of the common people the more natural the order and style seem to the English-speaking person. The speech of the uneducated freedmen in the romance of Petronius is interesting in this connection. They not only fail to use the period, but they rarely subordinate one idea to another. Instead of saying "I saw him when he was an ædile," they are likely to say "I saw him; he was an ædile then."

When we were analyzing preliterary Latin, we noticed that the co-ordination of ideas was one of its characteristics, so that this trait evidently persisted in popular speech, while literary Latin became more logical and complex.

In the preceding pages we have tried to find out the main features of popular Latin. In doing so we have constantly thought of literary Latin as the foil or standard of comparison. Now, strangely enough, no sooner had the literary medium of expression slowly and painfully disassociated itself from the language of the common people than influences which it could not resist brought it down again to the level of its humbler brother. Its integrity depended of course upon the acceptance of certain recognized standards. But when flourishing schools of literature sprang up in Spain, in Africa, and in Gaul, the paramount authority of Rome and the common standard for the Latin world which she had set were lost. When some men tried to imitate Cicero and Quintilian, and others, Seneca, there ceased to be a common model of excellence. Similarly a careful distinction between the diction of prose and verse was gradually obliterated. There was a loss of interest in literature, and professional writers gave less attention to their diction and style. The appearance of Christianity, too, exercised a profound influence on literary Latin. Christian writers and preachers made their appeal to the common people rather than to the literary world. They, therefore, expressed themselves in language which would be readily understood by the average man, as St. Jerome frankly tells us his purpose was. The result of these influences, and of others, acting on literary Latin, was to destroy its unity and its carefully developed scientific system, and to bring it nearer and nearer in its genius to popular Latin, or, to put it in another way, the literary medium comes to show many of the characteristics of the spoken language. Gregory of Tours, writing in the sixth century, laments the fact that he is unfamiliar with grammatical principles, and with this century literary Latin may be said to disappear.

As for popular Latin, it has never ceased to exist. It is the language of France, Spain, Italy, Roumania, and all the Romance countries today. Its history has been unbroken from the founding of Rome to the present time. Various scholars have tried to determine the date before which we shall call the popular speech vulgar Latin, and after which it may better be styled French or Spanish or Italian, as the case may be. Some would fix the dividing line in the early part of the eighth century A.D., when phonetic changes common to all parts of the Roman world would cease to occur. Others would fix it at different periods between the middle of the sixth to the middle of the seventh century, according as each section of the old Roman world passed definitely under the control of its Germanic invaders. The historical relations of literary and colloquial Latin would be roughly indicated by the accompanying diagram, in which preliterary Latin divides, on the appearance of literature in the third century B.C., into popular Latin and literary Latin. These two forms of speech develop along independent lines until, in the sixth century, literary Latin is merged in popular Latin and disappears. The unity for the Latin tongue thus secured was short lived, because within a century the differentiation begins which gives rise to the present-day Romance languages.

It may interest some of the readers of this chapter to look over a few specimens of vulgar Latin from the various periods of its history.

(a) The first one is an extract from the Laws of the Twelve Tables. The original document goes back to the middle of the fifth century B.C., and shows us some of the characteristics of preliterary Latin.

The non-periodic form, the omission of pronouns, and the change of subject without warning are especially noticeable.

"Si in ius vocat, ito. Ni it, antestamino, igitur em (=eum) capito. Si calvitur pedemve struit, manum endo iacito (=inicito). Si morbus aevitasve (=aetasve) vitium escit, iumentum dato: si nolet, arceram ne sternito."

1 Preliterary Latin.
2 Vulgar Latin
3 Literary Latin
4-8 The Romance languages.

(b) This passage from one of Cicero's letters to his brother (*ad Q. fr.* 2, 3, 2) may illustrate the familiar conversational style of a gentleman in the first century B.C. It describes an harangue made by the politician Clodius to his partisans.

"Ille furens et exsanguis interrogabat suos in clamore ipso quis esset qui plebem fame necaret. Respondebant operae: 'Pompeius.' Quem ire vellent. Respondebant: 'Crassum.' Is aderat tum Miloni animo non amico. Hora fere nona quasi signo dato Clodiani nostros consputare coeperunt. Exarsit dolor. Vrgere illi ut loco nos moverent."

(c) In the following passage, Petronius, 57, one of the freedmen at Trimalchio's dinner flames out in anger at a fellow-guest whose bearing seems to him supercilious. It shows a great many of the characteristics of vulgar Latin which have been mentioned in this paper. The similarity of its style to that of the preliterary specimen is worth observing. The great number of proverbs and bits of popular wisdom are also noticeable.

"Et nunc spero me sic vivere, ut nemini iocus sim. Homo inter homines sum, capite aperto ambulo; assem aerarium nemini debeo; constitutum habui nunquam; nemo mihi in foro dixit 'redde, quod debes.' Glebulas emi, lamelullas paravi; viginti ventres pasco et canem; contubernalem meam redemi, ne quis in sinu illius manus tergeret; mille denarios pro capite solvi; sevir gratis factus sum; spero, sic moriar, ut mortuus non erubescam."

(d) This short inscription from Pompeii shows some of the peculiarities of popular pronunciation. In ortu we see the same difficulty in knowing when to sound the aspirate which the cockney Englishman has. The silence of the final -m, and the reduction of ae to e are also interesting. Presta mi sinceru (=sincerum): si te amet que (=quae) custodit ortu (=hortum) Venus.

(e) Here follow some of the vulgar forms against which a grammarian, probably of the fourth century, warns his readers. We notice that the popular "mistakes" to which he calls attention are in (1) syncopation and assimilation, in (2) the use of the diminutive for the primitive, and pronouncing au as o, in (3) the same reduction of ct to t (or tt) which we find in such Romance forms as Ottobre, in (4) the aspirate falsely added, in (5) syncopation and the confusion of v and b, and in (6) the silence of final -m.

(1) frigida non fricda (2) auris non oricla (3) auctoritas non autoritas (4) ostiae non hostiae (5) vapulo non baplo (6) passim non passi

(f) The following passages are taken from Brunot's "Histoire de la langue Fraçaise," p. 144. In the third column the opening sentence of the famous Oath of Strasburg of 842 A.D. is given. In the other columns the form which it would have taken at different periods is set down. These passages bring out clearly the unbroken line of descent from Latin to modern French.

The Oath of Strasburg of 842

Classic Latin

Per Dei amorem et per christiani populi et nostram communem salutem, ab hac die, quantum Deus scire et posse mini dat, servabo hunc meum fratrem Carolum

Spoken Latin, Seventh Cent.

For deo amore et por chrestyano pob(o)lo et nostro comune salvamento de esto die en avante en quanto Deos sabere et podere me donat, sic salvarayo eo eccesto meon fradre Karlo

Actual Text

Pro deo amur et pro christian poblo et nostro commun salvament, d'ist di en avant, in quant Deus savir et podir me dunat, si salvarai eo cist meon fradre Karlo

French, Eleventh Cent.

Por dieu amor et por del crestüen poeple et nostre comun salvement, de cest jorn en avant, quant que Dieus saveir et podeir me donet, si salverai jo cest mien fredre Charlon

French, Fifteenth Cent.

Pour l'amour Dieu et pour le sauvement du chrestien peuple et le nostre commun, de cest jour en avant, quant que Dieu savoir et pouvoir me done, si sauverai je cest mien frere Charle

Modern French

Pour l'amour de Dieu et pour le salut commun du peuple chrétien et le nôtre, à partir de ce jour, autant que Dieu m'en donne le savoir et le pouvoir, je soutiendrai mon frère Charles

## The Poetry of the Common People of Rome

### I. Their Metrical Epitaphs

The old village churchyard on a summer afternoon is a favorite spot with many of us. The absence of movement, contrasted with the life just outside its walls, the drowsy humming of the bees in the flowers which grow at will, the restful gray of the stones and the green of the moss give one a feeling of peace and quiet, while the ancient dates and quaint lettering in the inscriptions carry us far from the hurry and bustle and trivial interests of present-day life. No sense of sadness touches us. The stories which the stones tell are so far removed from us in point of time that even those who grieved at the loss of the departed have long since followed their friends, and when we read the bits of life history on the crumbling monuments, we feel only that pleasurable emotion which, as Cicero says in one of his letters, comes from our reading in history of the little tragedies of men of the past. But the epitaph deals with the common people, whom history is apt to forget, and gives us a glimpse of their character, their doings, their beliefs, and their views of life and death. They furnish us a simple and direct record of the life and the aspirations of the average man, the record of a life not interpreted for us by the biographer, historian, or novelist, but set down in all its simplicity by one of the common people themselves.

These facts lend to the ancient Roman epitaphs their peculiar interest and charm. They give us a glimpse into the every-day life of the people which a Cicero, or a Virgil, or even a Horace cannot offer us. They must have exerted an influence, too, on Roman character, which we with our changed conditions can scarcely appreciate. We shall understand this fact if we call to mind the differences between the ancient practices in the matter of burial and our own. The village churchyard is with us a thing of the past. Whether on sanitary grounds, or for the sake of quiet and seclusion, in the interest of economy, or not to obtrude the thought of death upon us, the modern cemetery is put outside of our towns, and the memorials in it are rarely read by any of us. Our fathers did otherwise. The churchyard of old England and of New England was in the middle of the village, and "short cuts" from one part of the village to another led through its enclosure. Perhaps it was this fact which tempted our ancestors to set forth their life histories more fully than we do, who know that few, if any, will come to read them. Or is the world getting more reserved and sophisticated? Are we coming to put a greater restraint upon the expression of our emotions? Do we hesitate more than our fathers did to talk about ourselves? The ancient Romans were like our fathers in their willingness or desire to tell us of themselves. Perhaps the differences in their burial practices, which were mentioned above, tempted them to be communicative, and sometimes even garrulous. They put their tombstones in a spot still more frequented than the churchyard. They placed them by the side of the highways, just outside the city walls, where people were coming or going constantly. Along the Street of Tombs, as one goes out of Pompeii, or along the great Appian Way, which runs from Rome to Capua, Southern Italy and Brundisium, the port of departure for Greece and the Orient, they stand on both sides of the roadway and make their mute appeals for our attention. We know their like in the enclosure about old Trinity in New York, in the burial ground in New Haven, or in the churchyards across the water. They tell us not merely the date of birth and death of the deceased, but they let us know enough of his life to invest it with a certain individuality, and to give it a flavor of its own.

Some 40,000 of them have come down to us, and nearly 2,000 of the inscriptions upon them are metrical. This particular group is of special interest to us, because the use of verse seems to tempt the engraver to go beyond a bare statement of facts and to philosophize a bit about the present and the future. Those who lie beneath the stones still claim some recognition from the living, for they often call upon the passer-by to halt and read their epitaphs, and as the Roman walked along the Appian Way two thousand years ago, or as we stroll along the same highway to-day, it is in silent converse with the dead. Sometimes the stone itself addresses us, as does that of Olus Granius:[22] "This mute stone begs thee to stop, stranger, until it has disclosed its mission and told thee whose shade it covers. Here lie the bones of a man, modest, honest, and trusty--the crier, Olus Granius. That is all. It wanted thee not to be unaware of this. Fare thee well." This craving for the attention of the passer-by leads the composer of one epitaph to use somewhat the same device which our advertisers employ in the street-cars when they say: "Do not look at this spot," for he writes: "Turn not your eyes this way and wish not to learn our fate," but two lines later, relenting, he adds: "Now stop, traveller...within this narrow resting-place,"[23] and then we get the whole story. Sometimes a dramatic, lifelike touch is given by putting the inscription into the form of a dialogue between the dead and those who are left behind. Upon a stone found near Rome runs the inscription:[24] "Hail, name dear to us,

Stephanus,...thy Moschis and thy Diodorus salute thee." To which the dead man replies: "Hail chaste wife, hail Diodorus, my friend, my brother." The dead man often begs for a pleasant word from the passer-by. The Romans, for instance, who left Ostia by the highway, read upon a stone the sentiment:[25] "May it go well with you who lie within and, as for you who go your way and read these lines, 'the earth rest lightly on thee' say." This pious salutation loses some of the flavor of spontaneity in our eyes when we find that it had become so much of a convention as to be indicated by the initial letters of the several words: S(it) t(ibi) t(erra) l(evis). The traveller and the departed exchange good wishes on a stone found near Velitræ:[26]

"May it go well with you who read and you who pass this way, The like to mine and me who on this spot my tomb have built."

One class of passers-by was dreaded by the dweller beneath the stone--the man with a paint-brush who was looking for a conspicuous spot on which to paint the name of his favorite political candidate. To such an one the hope is expressed "that his ambition may be realized, provided he instructs his slave not to paint this stone."[27]

These wayside epitaphs must have left an impress on the mind and character of the Roman which we can scarcely appreciate. The peasant read them as he trudged homeward on market days, the gentleman, as he drove to his villa on the countryside, and the traveller who came from the South, the East, or the North. In them the history of his country was set forth in the achievements of her great men, her prætors and consuls, her generals who had conquered and her governors who had ruled Gaul, Spain, Africa, and Asia. In them the public services, and the deeds of charity of the rich and powerful were recorded and the homely virtues and self-sacrifices of the humbler man and woman found expression there. Check by jowl with the tomb of some great leader upon whom the people or the emperor had showered all the titles and honors in their power might stand the stone of the poor physician, Dionysius,[28] of whom it is said "to all the sick who came to him he gave his services free of charge; he set forth in his deeds what he taught in his precepts."

But perhaps more of the inscriptions in verse, and with them we are here concerned, are in praise of women than of men. They make clear to us the place which women held in Roman life, the state of society, and the feminine qualities which were held in most esteem. The world which they portray is quite another from that of Ovid and Juvenal. The common people still hold to the old standards of morality and duty. The degeneracy of smart society has made little progress here. The marriage tie is held sacred; the wife and husband, the parent and child are held close to each other in bonds of affection. The virtues of women are those which Martinianus records on the stone of his wife Sofroniola:[29]

"Purity, loyalty, affection, a sense of duty, a yielding nature, and whatever qualities God has implanted in women."

(Castitas fides earitas pietas obsequium Et quaecumque deus faemenis inesse praecepit.)

Upon a stone near Turin,[30] Valerius wrote in memory of his wife the simple line:

"Pure in heart, modest, of seemly bearing, discreet, noble-minded, and held in high esteem."

(Casta pudica decens sapiens Generosa probata.)

Only one discordant note is struck in this chorus of praise. This fierce invective stands upon an altar at Rome:[31] "Here for all time has been set down in writing the shameful record of the freedwoman Acte, of poisoned mind, and treacherous, cunning, and hard-hearted. Oh! for a nail, and a hempen rope to choke her, and flaming pitch to burn up her wicked heart."

A double tribute is paid to a certain Statilia in this naïve inscription:[32] "Thou who wert beautiful beyond measure and true to thy husbands, didst twice enter the bonds of wedlock...and he who came first, had he been able to withstand the fates, would have set up this stone to thee, while I, alas! who have been blessed by thy pure heart and love for thee for sixteen years, lo! now I have lost thee." Still greater sticklers for the truth at the expense of convention are two fond husbands who borrowed a pretty couplet composed in memory of some woman "of tender age," and then substituted upon the monuments of their wives the more truthful phrase "of middle age,"[33] and another man warns women, from the fate of his wife, to shun the excessive use of jewels.[34]

It was only natural that when men came to the end of life they should ask themselves its meaning, should speculate upon the state after death, and should turn their thoughts to the powers which controlled their destiny. We have been accustomed to form our conceptions of the religion of the Romans from what their philosophers and moralists and poets have written about it. But a great chasm lies between the teachings of these men and the beliefs of the common people. Only from a study of the epitaphs do we know what the average Roman thought and felt on this subject. A few years ago Professor Harkness, in an admirable article on "The Scepticism and Fatalism of the Common People of Rome," showed that "the common people placed no faith in the gods who occupy so prominent a place in Roman literature, and that their nearest approach to belief in a divinity was their recognition of fate," which "seldom appears as a fixed law of nature...but rather as a blind necessity, depending on chance and not on law." The gods are mentioned by name in the poetic epitaphs only, and for poetic purposes, and even here only one in fifty of the metrical inscriptions contains a direct reference to any supernatural power. For none of these deities, save for Mother Earth, does the writer of an epitaph show any affection. This feeling one may see in the couplet which reads:[35] "Mother Earth, to thee have we committed the bones of Fortunata, to thee who dost come near to thy children as a mother," and Professor Harkness thoughtfully remarks in this connection that "the love of nature and appreciation of its beauties, which form a distinguishing characteristic of Roman literature in contrast to all the other literatures of antiquity, are the outgrowth of this feeling of kinship which the Italians entertained for mother earth."

It is a little surprising, to us on first thought, that the Roman did not interpose some concrete personalities between himself and this vague conception of fate, some personal agencies, at least, to carry out the decrees of destiny. But it will not seem so strange after all when we recall the fact that the deities of the early Italians were without form or substance. The anthropomorphic teachings of Greek literature, art, and religion found an echo in the Jupiter and Juno, the Hercules and Pan of Virgil and Horace, but made no impress on the faith of the common people, who, with that regard for tradition which characterized the Romans, followed the fathers in their way of thinking.

A disbelief in personal gods hardly accords with faith in a life after death, but most of the Romans believed in an existence of some sort in the world beyond. A Dutch scholar has lately established this fact beyond reasonable doubt, by a careful study of the epitaphs in verse.[36] One tombstone reads:[37]

"Into nothing from nothing how quickly we go,"

and another:[38]

"Once we were not, now we are as we were,"

and the sentiment, "I was not, I was, I am not, I care not" (non fui, fui, non sum, non euro) was so freely used that it is indicated now and then merely by the initial letters N.f.f.n.s.n.c., but compared with the great number of inscriptions in which belief in a life after death finds expression such utterances are few. But how and where that life was to be passed the Romans were in doubt. We have noticed above how little the common people accepted the belief of the poets in Jupiter and Pluto and the other gods, or rather how little their theology had been influenced by Greek art and literature. In their conception of the place of abode after death, it is otherwise. Many of them believe with Virgil that it lies below the earth. As one of them says in his epitaph:[39]

"No sorrow to the world below I bring."

Or with other poets the departed are thought of as dwelling in the Elysian fields or the Isles of the Blessed. As one stone cries out to the passer-by:[40] "May you live who shall have said. 'She lives in Elysium,'" and of a little girl it is said:[41] "May thy shade flower in fields Elysian." Sometimes the soul goes to the sky or the stars: "Here lies the body of the bard Laberius, for his spirit has gone to the place from which it came;"[42] "The tomb holds my limbs, my soul shall pass to the stars of heaven."[43] But more frequently the departed dwell in the tomb. As one of them expresses it: "This is my eternal home; here have I been placed; here shall I be for aye." This belief that the shade hovers about the tomb accounts for the salutations addressed to it which we have noticed above, and for the food and flowers which are brought to satisfy its appetites and tastes. These tributes to the dead do not seem to accord with the current Roman belief that the body was dissolved to dust, and that the soul was clothed with some incorporeal form, but the Romans were no more consistent in their eschatology than many of us are.

Perhaps it was this vague conception of the state after death which deprived the Roman of that exultant joy in anticipation of the world beyond which the devout Christian, a hundred years or more ago, expressed in his epitaphs, with the Golden City so clearly pictured to his eye, and by way of compensation the Roman was saved from the dread of death, for no judgment-seat confronted him in the other world. The end of life was awaited with reasonable composure. Sometimes death was welcomed because it brought rest. As a citizen of Lambsesis expresses it:[44] "Here is my home forever; here is a rest from toil;" and upon a woman's stone we read:[45]

"Whither hast thou gone, dear soul, seeking rest from troubles, For what else than trouble hast thou had throughout thy life?"

But this pessimistic view of life rarely appears on the monuments. Not infrequently the departed expresses a certain satisfaction with his life's record, as does a citizen of Beneventum, who remarks:[46] "No man have I wronged, to many have I rendered services," or he tells us of the pleasure which he has found in the good things of life, and advises us to enjoy them. A Spanish epitaph reads:[47] "Eat, drink, enjoy thyself, follow me" (es bibe lude veni). In a lighter or more garrulous vein another says:[48] "Come, friends, let us enjoy the happy time of life; let us dine merrily, while short life lasts, mellow with wine, in jocund intercourse. All these about us did the same while they were living. They gave, received, and enjoyed good things while they lived. And let us imitate the practices of the fathers. Live while you live, and begrudge nothing to the dear soul which Heaven has given you." This philosophy of life is expressed very succinctly in: "What I have eaten and drunk I have with me; what I have foregone I have lost,"[49] and still more concretely in:

"Wine and amours and baths weaken our bodily health, Yet life is made up of wine and amours and baths."[50]

Under the statue of a man reclining and holding a cup in his hand, Flavius Agricola writes:[51] "Tibur was my native place; I was called Agricola, Flavius too.... I who lie here as you see me. And in the world above in the years which the fates granted, I cherished my dear soul, nor did the god of wine e'er fail me.... Ye friends who read this, I bid you mix your wine, and before death comes, crown your temples with flowers, and drink.... All the rest the earth and fire consume after death." Probably we should be wrong in tracing to the teachings of Epicurus, even in their vulgarized popular form, the theory that the value of life is to be estimated by the material pleasure it has to offer. A man's theory of life is largely a matter of temperament or constitution. He may find support for it in the teachings of philosophy, but he is apt to choose a philosophy which suits his way of thinking rather than to let his views of life be determined by abstract philosophic teachings. The men whose epitaphs we have just read would probably have been hedonists if Epicurus had never lived. It is interesting to note in passing that holding this conception of life naturally presupposes the acceptance of one of the notions of death which we considered above--that it ends all.

In another connection, a year or two ago, I had occasion to speak of the literary merit of some of these metrical epitaphs,[52] of their interest for us as specimens of the literary compositions of the common people, and of their value in indicating the æsthetic taste of the average Roman. It may not be without interest here to speak of the literary form of some of them a little more at length than was possible in that connection. Latin has always been, and continues to be among modern peoples, a favored language for epitaphs and dedications. The reasons why it holds its favored position are not far to seek. It is vigorous and concise. Then again in English and in most modern languages the order which words may take in a given sentence is in most cases inexorably fixed by grammatical necessity. It was not so with Latin. Its highly inflected character made it possible, as we know, to arrange the words which convey an idea in various orders, and these different groupings of the same words gave different shades of meaning to the sentence, and different emotional effects are secured by changing the sequence in which the minor conceptions are presented. By putting contrasted words side by side, or at corresponding points in the sentence, the impression is heightened. When a composition takes the form of verse the possibilities in the way of contrast are largely increased. The high degree of perfection to which Horace brought the balancing and interlocking of ideas in some of his Odes, illustrates the great advantage which the Latin poet had over the English writer because of the flexibility of the medium of expression which he used. This advantage was the Roman's birthright, and lends a certain distinction even to the verses of the people, which we are discussing here. Certain other stylistic qualities of these metrical epitaphs, which are intended to produce somewhat the same effects, will not seem to us so admirable. I mean alliteration, play upon words, the acrostic arrangement, and epigrammatic effects. These literary tricks find little place in our serious verse, and the finer Latin poets rarely indulge in them. They seem to be especially out of place in an epitaph, which should avoid studied effects and meretricious devices. But writers in the early stages of a literature and common people of all periods find a pleasure in them. Alliteration, onomatopœia, the pun, and the play on words are to be found in all the early Latin poets, and they are especially frequent with literary men like Plautus and Terence, Pacuvius and Accius, who wrote for the stage, and therefore for the common people. One or two illustrations of the use of these literary devices may be sufficient. A little girl at Rome, who died when five years old, bore the strange name of Mater, or Mother, and on her tombstone stands the sentiment:[53] "Mater I was by name, mater I shall not be by law." "Sepulcrum hau pulcrum pulcrai feminae" of the famous Claudia inscription,[54] Professor Lane cleverly rendered "Site not sightly of a sightly dame." Quite beyond my power of translating into English, so as to reproduce its complicated play on words, is the appropriate epitaph of the rhetorician, Romanius lovinus:[55]

"Docta loqui doctus quique loqui docuit."

A great variety of verses is used in the epitaphs, but the dactylic hexameter and the elegiac are the favorites. The stately character of the hexameter makes it a suitable medium in which to express a serious sentiment, while the sudden break in the second verse of the elegiac couplet suggests the emotion of the writer. The verses are constructed with considerable regard for technique. Now and then there is a false quantity, an unpleasant sequence, or a heavy effect, but such blemishes are comparatively infrequent. There is much that is trivial, commonplace, and prosaic in these productions of the common people, but now and then one comes upon a phrase, a verse, or a whole poem which shows strength or grace or pathos. An orator of the late period, not without vigor, writes upon his tombstone:[56] "I have lived blessed by the gods, by friends, by letters."

(Vixi beatus dis, amicis, literis.)

A rather pretty, though not unusual, sentiment occurs in an elegiac couplet to a young girl,[57] in which the word amoena is the adjective, meaning "pleasant to see," in the first, while in the second verse it is the girl's name: "As a rose is amoena when it blooms in the early spring time, so was I Amoena to those who saw me."

(Ut rosa amoena homini est quom primo tempore floret. Quei me viderunt, seic Amoena fui.)

There is a touch of pathos in the inscription which a mother put on the stone of her son:[58] "A sorrowing mother has set up this monument to a son who has never caused her any sorrow, except that he is no more," and in this tribute of a husband:[59] "Out of my slender means now that the end has come, my wife, all that I could do, this gift, a small small one for thy deserts, have I made." The epitaph of a little girl, named Felicia, or Kitty, has this sentiment in graceful verse:[60] "Rest lightly upon thee the earth, and over thy grave the fragrant balsam grow, and roses sweet entwine thy buried bones." Upon the stone of a little girl who bore the name of Xanthippe, and the nickname Iaia, is an inscription with one of two pretty conceits and phrases. With it we may properly bring to an end our brief survey of these verses of the common people of Rome. In a somewhat free rendering it reads in part:[61] "Whether the thought of death distress thee or of life, read to the end. Xanthippe by name, yclept also Iaia by way of jest, escapes from sorrow since her soul from the body flies. She rests here in the soft cradle of the earth,... comely, charming, keen of mind, gay in discourse. If there be aught of compassion in the gods above, bear her to the sun and light."

## The Common People of Ancient Rome

### II. Their Dedicatory and Ephemeral Verses

In the last paper we took up for consideration some of the Roman metrical epitaphs. These compositions, however, do not include all the productions in verse of the common people of Rome. On temples, altars, bridges, statues, and house walls, now and then, we find bits of verse. Most of the extant dedicatory lines are in honor of Hercules, Silvanus, Priapus, and the Cæsars. Whether the two famous inscriptions to Hercules by the sons of Vertuleius and by Mummius belong here or not it is hard to say. At all events, they were probably composed by amateurs, and have a peculiar interest for us because they belong to the second century B.C., and therefore stand near the beginning of Latin letters; they show us the language before it had been perfected and adapted to literary purposes by an Ennius, a Virgil, and a Horace, and they are written in the old native Saturnian verse, into which Livius Andronicus, "the Father of Latin literature," translated the Odyssey. Consequently they show us the language before it had gained in polish and lost in vigor under the influence of the Greeks. The second of these two little poems is a finger-post, in fact, at the parting of the ways for Roman civilization. It was upon a tablet let into the wall of the temple of Hercules, and commemorates the triumphant return to Rome of Mummius, the conqueror of Corinth. It points back to the good old days of Roman contempt for Greek art, and ignorance of it, for Mummius, in his stupid indifference to the beautiful monuments of Corinth, made himself the typical Philistine for all time. It points forward to the new Greco-Roman civilization of Italy, because the works of art which Mummius is said to have brought back with him, and the Greeks who probably followed in his train, augmented that stream of Greek influence which in the next century or two swept through the peninsula.

In the same primitive metre as these dedications is the Song of the Arval Brothers, which was found engraved on a stone in the grove of the goddess Dea Dia, a few miles outside of Rome. This hymn the priests sang at the May festival of the goddess, when the farmers brought them the first fruits of the earth. It has no intrinsic literary merit, but it carries us back beyond the great wars with Carthage for supremacy in the western Mediterranean, beyond the contest with Pyrrhus for overlordship in Southern Italy, beyond the struggle for life with the Samnites in Central Italy, beyond even the founding of the city on the Tiber, to a people who lived by tilling the soil and tending their flocks and herds.

But we have turned away from the dedicatory verses. On the bridges which span our streams we sometimes record the names of the commissioners or the engineers, or the bridge builders responsible for the structure. Perhaps we are wise in thinking these prosaic inscriptions suitable for our ugly iron bridges. Their more picturesque stone structures tempted the Romans now and then to drop into verse, and to go beyond a bare statement of the facts of construction. Over the Anio in Italy, on a bridge which Narses, the great general of Justinian, restored, the Roman, as he passed, read in graceful verse:[62] "We go on our way with the swift-moving waters of the torrent beneath our feet, and we delight on hearing the roar of the angry water. Go then joyfully at your ease, Quirites, and let the echoing murmur of the stream sing ever of Narses. He who could subdue the unyielding spirit of the Goths has taught the rivers to bear a stern yoke."

It is an interesting thing to find that the prettiest of the dedicatory poems are in honor of the forest-god Silvanus. One of these poems, Titus Pomponius Victor, the agent of the Cæsars, left inscribed upon a tablet[63] high up in the Grecian Alps. It reads: "Silvanus, half-enclosed in the sacred ash-tree, guardian mighty art thou of this pleasaunce in the heights. To thee we consecrate in verse these thanks, because across the fields and Alpine tops, and through thy guests in sweetly smelling groves, while justice I dispense and the concerns of Cæsar serve, with thy protecting care thou guidest us. Bring me and mine to Rome once more, and grant that we may till Italian fields with thee as guardian. In guerdon therefor will I give a thousand mighty trees." It is a pretty picture. This deputy of Cæsar has finished his long and perilous journeys through the wilds of the North in the performance of his duties. His face is now turned toward Italy, and his thoughts are fixed on Rome. In this "little garden spot," as he calls it, in the mountains he pours out his gratitude to the forest-god, who has carried him safely through dangers and brought him thus far on his homeward way, and he vows a thousand trees to his protector. It is too bad that we do not know how the vow was to be paid--not by cutting down the trees, we feel sure. One line of Victor's little poem is worth quoting in the original. He thanks Silvanus for conducting him in safety "through the mountain heights, and through Tuique luci suave olentis hospites." Who are the *hospites*? The wild beasts of the forests, we suppose. Now *hospites* may, of course, mean either "guests" or "hosts," and it is a pretty conceit of Victor's to think of the wolves and bears as the guests of the forest-god, as we have ventured to render the phrase in the translation given above. Or, are they Victor's hosts, whose characters have been so changed by Silvanus that Victor has had friendly help rather than fierce attacks from them?

A very modern practice is revealed by a stone found near the famous temple of Æsculapius, the god of healing, at Epidaurus in Argolis, upon which two ears are shown in relief, and below them the Latin couplet:[64] "Long ago Cutius Gallus had vowed these ears to thee, scion of Phœbus, and now he has put them here, for thou hast healed his ears." It is an ancient ex-voto, and calls to mind on the one hand the cult of Æsculapius, which Walter Pater has so charmingly portrayed in Marius the Epicurean, and on the other hand it shows us that the practice of setting up ex-votos, of which one sees so many at shrines and in churches across the water to-day, has been borrowed from the pagans. A pretty bit of sentiment is suggested by an inscription[65] found near the ancient village of Ucetia in Southern France: "This shrine to the Nymphs have I built, because many times and oft have I used this spring when an old man as well as a youth."

All of the verses which we have been considering up to this point have come down to us more or less carefully engraved upon stone, in honor of some god, to record some achievement of importance, or in memory of a departed friend. But besides these formal records of the past, we find a great many hastily scratched or painted sentiments or notices, which have a peculiar interest for us because they are the careless effusions or unstudied productions of the moment, and give us the atmosphere of antiquity as nothing else can do. The stuccoed walls of the houses, and the sharp-pointed stylus which was used in writing on wax tablets offered too strong a temptation for the lounger or passer-by to resist. To people of this class, and to merchants advertising their wares, we owe the three thousand or more graffiti found at Pompeii. The ephemeral inscriptions which were intended for practical purposes, such as the election notices, the announcements of gladiatorial contests, of houses to rent, of articles lost and for sale, are in prose, but the lovelorn lounger inscribed his sentiments frequently in verse, and these verses deserve a passing notice here. One man of this class in his erotic ecstasy writes on the wall of a Pompeian basilica:[66] "May I perish if I'd wish to be a god without thee." That hope sprang eternal in the breast of the Pompeian lover is illustrated by the last two lines of this tragic declaration:[67]

"If you can and won't, Give me hope no more. Hope you foster and you ever Bid me come again to-morrow. Force me then to die Whom you force to live A life apart from you. Death will be a boon, Not to be tormented. Yet what hope has snatched away To the lover hope gives back."

This effusion has led another passer-by to write beneath it the Delphic sentiment: "May the man who shall read this never read anything else." The symptoms of the ailment in its most acute form are described by some Roman lover in the verses which he has left us on the wall of Caligula's palace, on the Palatine:[68]

"No courage in my heart, No sleep to close my eyes, A tide of surging love Throughout the day and night."

This seems to come from one who looks upon the lover with a sympathetic eye, but who is himself fancy free:

"Whoever loves, good health to him, And perish he who knows not how, But doubly ruined may he be Who will not yield to love's appeal."[69]

The first verse of this little poem,

"Quisquis amat valeat, pereat qui nescit amare,"

represented by the first couplet of the English rendering, calls to mind the swinging refrain which we find a century or two later in the *Pervigilium Veneris*, that last lyrical outburst of the pagan world, written for the eve of the spring festival of Venus:

"Cras amet qui nunquam amavit quique amavit eras amet."

(To-morrow he shall love who ne'er has loved And who has loved, to-morrow he shall love.)

An interesting study might be made of the favorite types of feminine beauty in the Roman poets. Horace sings of the "golden-haired" Pyrrhas, and Phyllises, and Chloes, and seems to have had an admiration for blondes, but a poet of the common people, who has recorded his opinion on this subject in the atrium of a Pompeian house, shows a more catholic taste, although his freedom of judgment is held in some constraint:

"My fair girl has taught me to hate Brunettes with their tresses of black. I will hate if I can, but if not, 'Gainst my will I must love them also."[70]

On the other hand, one Pompeian had such an inborn dread of brunettes that, whenever he met one, he found it necessary to take an appropriate antidote, or prophylactic:

"Whoever loves a maiden dark By charcoal dark is he consumed. When maiden dark I light upon I eat the saving blackberry."[71]

These amateur poets do not rely entirely upon their own Muse, but borrow from Ovid, Propertius, or Virgil, when they recall sentiments in those writers which express their feelings. Sometimes it is a tag, or a line, or a couplet which is taken, but the borrowings are woven into the context with some skill. The poet above who is under compulsion from his blonde sweetheart, has taken the second half of his production verbatim from Ovid, and for the first half of it has modified a line of Propertius. Other writers have set down their sentiments in verse on more prosaic subjects. A traveller on his way to the capital has scribbled these lines on the wall, perhaps of a wine-shop where he stopped for refreshment:[72]

"Hither have we come in safety. Now I hasten on my way, That once more it may be mine To behold our Lares, Rome."

At one point in a Pompeian street, the eye of a straggler would catch this notice in doggerel verse:[73]

"Here's no place for loafers. Lounger, move along!"

On the wall of a wine-shop a barmaid has thus advertised her wares:[74]

"Here for a cent is a drink, Two cents brings something still better. Four cents in all, if you pay, Wine of Falernum is yours."

It must have been a lineal descendant of one of the parasites of Plautus who wrote:[75]

"A barbarian he is to me At whose house I'm not asked to dine."

Here is a sentiment which sounds very modern:

"The common opinion is this: That property should be divided."[76]

This touch of modernity reminds one of another group of verses which brings antiquity into the closest possible touch with some present-day practices. The Romans, like ourselves, were great travellers and sightseers, and the marvels of Egypt in particular appealed to them, as they do to us, with irresistible force. Above all, the great statue of Memnon, which gave forth a strange sound when it was struck by the first rays of the rising sun, drew travellers from far and near. Those of us who know the Mammoth Cave, Niagara Falls, the Garden of the Gods, or some other of our natural wonders, will recall how fond a certain class of visitors are of immortalizing themselves by scratching their names or a sentiment on the walls or the rocks which form these marvels. Such inscriptions We find on the temple walls in Egypt--three of them appear on the statue of Memnon, recording in verse the fact that the writers had visited the statue and heard the voice of the god at sunrise. One of these Egyptian travellers, a certain Roman lady journeying up the Nile, has scratched these verses on a wall of the temple at Memphis:[77]

"The pyramids without thee have I seen, My brother sweet, and yet, as tribute sad, The bitter tears have poured adown my cheek, And sadly mindful of thy absence now I chisel here this melancholy note."

Then follow the name and titles of the absent brother, who is better known to posterity from these scribbled lines of a Cook's tourist than from any official records which have come down to us. All of these pieces of popular poetry which we have been discussing thus far were engraved on stone, bronze, stucco, or on some other durable material. A very few bits of this kind of verse, from one to a half dozen lines in length, have come down to us in literature. They have the unique distinction, too, of being specimens of Roman folk poetry, and some of them are found in the most unlikely places. Two of them are preserved by a learned commentator on the Epistles of Horace. They carry us back to our school-boy days. When we read

"The plague take him who's last to reach me,"[78]

we can see the Roman urchin standing in the market-place, chanting the magic formula, and opposite him the row of youngsters on tiptoe, each one waiting for the signal to run across the intervening space and be the first to touch their comrade. What visions of early days come back to us--days when we clasped hands in a circle and danced about one or two children placed in the centre of the ring, and chanted in unison some refrain, upon reading in the same commentator to Horace a ditty which runs:[79]

"King shall you be If you do well. If you do ill You shall not be."

The other bits of Roman folk poetry which we have are most of them preserved by Suetonius, the gossipy biographer of the Cæsars. They recall very different scenes. Cæsar has returned in triumph to Rome, bringing in his train the trousered Gauls, to mingle on the street with the toga-clad Romans. He has even had the audacity to enroll some of these strange peoples in the Roman senate, that ancient body of dignity and convention, and the people chant in the streets the ditty:[80]

"Cæsar leads the Gauls in triumph, In the senate too he puts them. Now they've donned the broad-striped toga And have laid aside their breeches."

Such acts as these on Cæsar's part led some political versifier to write on Cæsar's statue a couplet which contrasted his conduct with that of the first great republican, Lucius Brutus:

"Brutus drove the kings from Rome, And first consul thus became. This man drove the consuls out, And at last became the king."[81]

We may fancy that these verses played no small part in spurring on Marcus Brutus to emulate his ancestor and join the conspiracy against the tyrant. With one more bit of folk poetry, quoted by Suetonius, we may bring our sketch to an end. Germanicus Cæsar, the flower of the imperial family, the brilliant general and idol of the people, is suddenly stricken with a mortal illness. The crowds throng the streets to hear the latest news from the sick-chamber of their hero. Suddenly the rumor flies through the streets that the crisis is past, that Germanicus will live, and the crowds surge through the public squares chanting:

"Saved now is Rome, Saved too the land, Saved our Germanicus."[82]

## The Origin of the Realistic Romance among the Romans

One of the most fascinating and tantalizing problems of literary history concerns the origin of prose fiction among the Romans. We can trace the growth of the epic from its infancy in the third century before Christ as it develops in strength in the poems of Nævius, Ennius, and Cicero until it reaches its full stature in the *Æneid,* and then we can see the decline of its vigor in the *Pharsalia,* the *Punica,* the *Thebais,* and *Achilleis,* until it practically dies a natural death in the mythological and historical poems of Claudian. The way also in which tragedy, comedy, lyric poetry, history, biography, and the other types of literature in prose and verse came into existence and developed among the Romans can be followed with reasonable success. But the origin and early history of the novel is involved in obscurity. The great realistic romance of Petronius of the first century of our era is without a legally recognized ancestor and has no direct descendant. The situation is the more surprising when we recall its probable size in its original form. Of course only a part of it has come down to us, some one hundred and ten pages in all. Its great size probably proved fatal to its preservation in its complete form, or at least contributed to that end, for it has been estimated that it ran from six hundred to nine hundred pages, being longer, therefore, than the average novel of Dickens and Scott. Consequently we are not dealing with a bit of ephemeral literature, but with an elaborate composition of a high degree of excellence, behind which we should expect to find a long line of development. We are puzzled not so much by the utter absence of anything in the way of prose fiction before the time of Petronius as by the difficulty of establishing any satisfactory logical connection between these pieces of literature and the romance of Petronius. We are bewildered, in fact, by the various possibilities which the situation presents. The work shows points of similarity with several antecedent forms of composition, but the gaps which lie in any assumed line of descent are so great as to make us question its correctness.

If we call to mind the present condition of this romance and those characteristic features of it which are pertinent to the question at issue, the nature of the problem and its difficulty also will be apparent at once. Out of the original work, in a rather fragmentary form, only four or five main episodes are extant, one of which is the brilliant story of the Dinner of Trimalchio. The action takes place for the most part in Southern Italy, and the principal characters are freedmen who have made their fortunes and degenerate freemen who are picking up a precarious living by their wits. The freemen, who are the central figures in the novel, are involved in a great variety of experiences, most of them of a disgraceful sort, and the story is a story of low life. Women play an important rôle in the narrative, more important perhaps than they do in any other kind of ancient literature--at least their individuality is more marked. The efficient motif is erotic. I say the efficient, because the conventional motif which seems to account for all the misadventures of the anti-hero Encolpius is the wrath of an offended deity. A great part of the book has an atmosphere of satire about it which piques our curiosity and baffles us at the same time, because it is hard to say how much of this element is inherent in the subject itself, and how much of it lies in the intention of the author. It is the characteristic of parvenu society to imitate smart society to the best of its ability, and its social functions are a parody of the like events in the upper set. The story of a dinner party, for instance, given by such a *nouveau riche* as Trimalchio, would constantly remind us by its likeness and its unlikeness, by its sins of omission and commission, of a similar event in correct society. In other words, it would be a parody on a proper dinner, even if the man who described the event knew nothing about the usages of good society, and with no ulterior motive in mind set down accurately the doings of his upstart characters. For instance, when Trimalchio's chef has three white pigs driven into the dining-room for the ostensible purpose of allowing the guests to pick one out for the next course, with the memory of our own monkey breakfasts and horseback dinners in mind, we may feel that this is a not improbable attempt on the part of a Roman parvenu to imitate his betters in giving a dinner somewhat out of the ordinary. Members of the smart set at Rome try to impress their guests by the value and weight of their silver plate. Why shouldn't the host of our story adopt the more direct and effective way of accomplishing the same object by having the weight of silver engraved on each article? He does so. It is a very natural thing for him to do. In good society they talk of literature and art. Why isn't it natural for Trimalchio to turn the conversation into the same channels, even if he does make Hannibal take Troy and does confuse the epic heroes and some late champions of the gladiatorial ring?

In other words, much of that which is satirical in Petronius is so only because we are setting up in our minds a comparison between the doings of his rich freedmen and the requirements of good taste and moderation. But it seems possible to detect a satirical or a cynical purpose on the part of the author carried farther than is involved in the choice of his subject and the realistic presentation of his characters. Petronius seems to delight in putting his most admirable sentiments in the mouths of contemptible characters. Some of the best literary criticism we have of the period, he presents through the medium of the parasite rhetorician Agamemnon. That happy phrase characterizing Horace's style, "curiosa felicitas," which has perhaps never been equalled in its brevity and appositeness, is coined by the incorrigible poetaster Eumolpus. It is he too who composes and recites the two rather brilliant epic poems incorporated into the *Satirae*, one of which is received with a shower of stones by the bystanders. The impassioned eulogy of the careers of Democritus, Chrysippus, Lysippus, and Myron, who had endured hunger, pain, and weariness of body and mind for the sake of science, art, and the good of their fellow-men, and the diatribe against the pursuit of comfort and pleasure which characterized the people of his own time, are put in the mouth of the same *roué* Eumolpus.

These situations have the true Horatian humor about them. The most serious and systematic discourse which Horace has given us, in his Satires, on the art of living, comes from the crack-brained Damasippus, who has made a failure of his own life. In another of his poems, after having set forth at great length the weaknesses of his fellow-mortals, Horace himself is convicted of being inconsistent, a slave to his passions, and a victim of hot temper by his own slave Davus. We are reminded again of the literary method of Horace in his Satires when we read the dramatic description of the shipwreck in Petronius. The blackness of night descends upon the water; the little bark which contains the hero and his friends is at the mercy of the sea; Lichas, the master of the vessel, is swept from the deck by a wave, Encolpius and his comrade Giton prepare to die in each other's embrace, but the tragic scene ends with a ridiculous picture of Eumolpus bellowing out above the roar of the storm a new poem which he is setting down upon a huge piece of parchment. Evidently Petronius has the same dread of being taken too seriously which Horace shows so often in his Satires. The cynical, or at least unmoral, attitude of Petronius is brought out in a still more marked way at the close of this same passage. Of those upon the ill-fated ship the degenerates Encolpius, Giton, and Eumolpus, who have wronged Lichas irreparably, escape, while the pious Lichas meets a horrible death. All this seems to make it clear that not only does the subject which Petronius has treated inevitably involve a satire upon contemporary society, but that the author takes a satirical or cynical attitude toward life.

Another characteristic of the story is its realism. There are no marvellous adventures, and in fact no improbable incidents in it. The author never obtrudes his own personality upon us, as his successor Apuleius sometimes does, or as Thackeray has done. We know what the people in the story are like, not from the author's description of them, but from their actions, from the subjects about which they talk, and from the way in which they talk. Agamemnon converses as a rhetorician might talk, Habinnas like a millionnaire stone-cutter, and Echion like a rag-dealer, and their language and style are what we should expect from men of their standing in society and of their occupations. The conversations of Trimalchio and his freedmen guests are not witty, and their jests are not clever. This adherence to the true principles of realism is the more noteworthy in the case of so brilliant a writer as Petronius, and those of us who recall some of the preternaturally clever conversations in the pages of Henry James and other contemporary novelists may feel that in this respect he is a truer artist than they are.

The novel of Petronius has one other characteristic which is significant, if we attempt to trace the origin of this type of literature. It is cast in the prose-poetic form, that is, passages in verse are inserted here and there in the narrative. In a few cases they are quoted, but for the most part they are the original compositions of the novelist. They range in length from couplets to poems of three hundred lines. Sometimes they form an integral part of the narrative, or again they illustrate a point, elaborate an idea in poetry, or are exercises in verse.

We have tried to bring out the characteristic features of this romance in order that we may see what the essential elements are of the problem which faces one in attempting to explain the origin of the type of literature represented by the work of Petronius. What was there in antecedent literature which will help us to understand the appearance on Italian soil in the first century of our era of a long erotic story of adventure, dealing in a realistic way with every-day life, marked by a satirical tone and with a leaning toward the prose-poetic form? This is the question raised by the analysis, which we have made above, of the characteristics of the story. We have no ambitious hope of solving it, yet the mere statement of a puzzling but interesting problem is stimulating to the imagination and the intellect, and I am tempted to take up the subject because the discovery of certain papyri in Egypt within recent years has led to the formulation of a new theory of the origin of the romance of perilous adventure, and may, therefore, throw some light on the source of our realistic novel of every-day life. My purpose, then, is to speak briefly of the different genres of literature of the earlier period with which the story of Petronius may stand in some direct relation, or from which the suggestion may have come to Petronius for his work. Several of these lines of possible descent have been skilfully traced by others. In their views here and there I have made some modifications, and I have called attention to one or two types of literature, belonging to the earlier period and heretofore unnoticed in this connection, which may help us to understand the appearance of the realistic novel.

It seems a far cry from this story of sordid motives and vulgar action to the heroic episodes of epic poetry, and yet the *Satirae* contain not a few more or less direct suggestions of epic situations and characters. The conventional motif of the story of Petronius is the wrath of an offended deity. The narrative in the *Odyssey* and the *Æneid* rests on the same basis. The ship of their enemy Lichas on which Encolpius and his companions are cooped up reminds them of the cave of the Cyclops; Giton hiding from the town-crier under a mattress is compared to Ulysses underneath the sheep and clinging to its wool to escape the eye of the Cyclops, while the woman whose charms engage the attention of Encolpius at Croton bears the name of Circe. It seems to be clear from these reminiscences that Petronius had the epic in mind when he wrote his story, and his novel may well be a direct or an indirect parody of an epic narrative. Rohde in his analysis of the serious Greek romance of the centuries subsequent to Petronius has postulated the following development for that form of story: Travellers returning from remote parts of the world told remarkable stories of their experiences. Some of these stories took a literary form in the *Odyssey* and the Tales of the Argonauts. They appeared in prose, too, in narratives like the story of Sinbad the Sailor, of a much later date. A more definite plot and a greater dramatic intensity were given to these tales of adventure by the addition of an erotic element which often took the form of two separated lovers. Some use is made of this element, for instance, in the relations of Odysseus and Penelope, perhaps in the episode of Æneas and Dido, and in the story of Jason and Medea. The intrusion of the love motif into the stories told of demigods and heroes, so that the whole narrative turns upon it, is illustrated by such tales in the Metamorphoses of Ovid as those of Pyramus and Thisbe, Pluto and Proserpina, or Meleager and Atalanta. The love element, which may have been developed in this way out of its slight use in the epic, and the element of adventure form the basis of the serious Greek romances of Antonius Diogenes, Achilles Tatius, and the other writers of the centuries which follow Petronius.

Before trying to connect the *Satirae* with a serious romance of the type just mentioned, let us follow another line of descent which leads us to the same objective point, viz., the appearance of the serious story in prose. We have been led to consider the possible connection of this kind of prose fiction with the epic by the presence in both of them of the love element and that of adventure. But the Greek novel has another rather marked feature. It is rhetorical, and this quality has suggested that it may have come, not from the epic, but from the rhetorical exercise. Support has been given to this theory within recent years by the discovery in Egypt of two fragments of the Ninos romance. The first of these fragments reveals Ninos, the hero, pleading with his aunt Derkeia, the mother of his sweetheart, for permission to marry his cousin. All the arguments in support of his plea and against it are put forward and balanced one against the other in a very systematic way. He wins over Derkeia. Later in the same fragment the girl pleads in a somewhat similar fashion with Thambe, the mother of Ninos. The second fragment is mainly concerned with the campaigns of Ninos. Here we have the two lovers, probably separated by the departure of Ninos for the wars, while the hero, at least, is exposed to the danger of the campaign.

The point was made after the text of this find had been published that the large part taken in the tale by the carefully balanced arguments indicated that the story grew out of exercises in argumentation in the rhetorical schools.[83] The elder Seneca has preserved for us in his *Controversiae* specimens of the themes which were set for students in these schools. The student was asked to imagine himself in a supposed dilemma and then to discuss the considerations which would lead him to adopt the one or the other line of conduct. Some of these situations suggest excellent dramatic possibilities, conditions of life, for instance, where suicide seemed justifiable, misadventures with pirates, or a turn of affairs which threatened a woman's virtue. Before the student reached the point of arguing the case, the story must be told, and out of these narratives of adventure, told at the outset to develop the dilemma, may have grown the romance of adventure, written for its own sake. The story of Ninos has a peculiar interest in connection with this theory, because it was probably very short, and consequently may give us the connecting link between the rhetorical exercise and the long novel of the later period, and because it is the earliest known serious romance. On the back of the papyrus which contains it are some farm accounts of the year 101 A.D. Evidently by that time the roll had become waste paper, and the story itself may have been composed a century or even two centuries earlier. So far as this second theory is concerned, we may raise the question in passing whether we have any other instance of a genre of literature growing out of a school-boy exercise. Usually the teacher adapts to his purpose some form of creative literature already in existence.

Leaving this objection out of account for the moment, the romance of love and perilous adventure may possibly be then a lineal descendant either of the epic or of the rhetorical exercise. Whichever of these two views is the correct one, the discovery of the Ninos romance fills in a gap in one theory of the origin of the realistic romance of Petronius, and with that we are here concerned. Before the story of Ninos was found, no serious romance and no title of such a romance anterior to the time of Petronius was known. This story, as we have seen, may well go back to the first century before Christ, or at least to the beginning of our era. It is conceivable that stories like it, but now lost, existed even at an earlier date. Now in the century, more or less, which elapsed between the assumed date of the appearance of these Greek narratives and the time of Petronius, the extraordinary commercial development of Rome had created a new aristocracy--the aristocracy of wealth. In harmony with this social change the military chieftain and the political leader who had been the heroes of the old fiction gave way to the substantial man of affairs of the new, just as Thaddeus of Warsaw has yielded his place in our present-day novels to Silas Lapham, and the bourgeois erotic story of adventure resulted, as we find it in the extant Greek novels of the second and third centuries of our era. If we can assume that this stage of development was reached before the time of Petronius we can think of his novel as a parody of such a romance. If, however, the bourgeois romance had not appeared before 50 A.D., then, if we regard his story as a parody of a prose narrative, it must be a parody of such an heroic romance as that of Ninos, or a parody of the longer heroic romances which developed out of the rhetorical narrative. If excavations in Egypt or at Herculaneum should bring to light a serious bourgeois story of adventure, they would furnish us the missing link. Until, or unless, such a discovery is made the chain of evidence is incomplete.

The two theories of the realistic romance which we have been discussing assume that it is a parody of some anterior form of literature, and that this fact accounts for the appearance of the satirical or cynical element in it. Other students of literary history, however, think that this characteristic was brought over directly from the Milesian tale[84] or the Menippean satire.[85] To how many different kinds of stories the term "Milesian tale" was applied by the ancients is a matter of dispute, but the existence of the short story before the time of Petronius is beyond question. Indeed we find specimens of it. In its commonest form it presented a single episode of every-day life. It brought out some human weakness or foible. Very often it was a story of illicit love. Its philosophy of life was: No man's honesty and no woman's virtue are unassailable. In all these respects, save in the fact that it presents one episode only, it resembles the *Satirae* of Petronius. At least two stories of this type are to be found in the extant fragments of the novel of Petronius. One of them is related as a well-known tale by the poet Eumolpus, and the other is told by him as a personal experience. More than a dozen of them are imbedded in the novel of Apuleius, the *Metamorphoses,* and modern specimens of them are to be seen in Boccaccio and in Chaucer. In fact they are popular from the twelfth century down to the eighteenth. Long before the time of Petronius they occur sporadically in literature. A good specimen, for instance, is found in a letter commonly attributed to Æschines in the fourth century B.C. As early as the first century before Christ collections of them had been made and translated into Latin. This development suggests an interesting possible origin of the realistic romance. In such collections as those just mentioned of the first century B.C., the central figures were different in the different stories, as is the case, for instance, in the Canterbury Tales. Such an original writer as Petronius was may well have thought of connecting these different episodes by making them the experiences of a single individual. The Encolpius of Petronius would in that case be in a way an ancient Don Juan. If we compare the Arabian Nights with one of the groups of stories found in the Romances of the Round Table, we can see what this step forward would mean. The tales which bear the title of the Arabian Nights all have the same general setting and the same general treatment, and they are put in the mouth of the same story-teller. The Lancelot group of Round Table stories, however, shows a nearer approach to unity since the stories in it concern the same person, and have a common ultimate purpose, even if it is vague. When this point had been reached the realistic romance would have made its appearance. We have been thinking of the realistic novel as being made up of a series of Milesian tales. We may conceive of it, however, as an expanded Milesian tale, just as scholars are coming to think of the epic as growing out of a single hero-song, rather than as resulting from the union of several such songs.

To pass to another possibility, it is very tempting to see a connection between the *Satirae* of Petronius and the prologue of comedy. Plautus thought it necessary to prefix to many of his plays an account of the incidents which preceded the action of the play. In some cases he went so far as to outline in the prologue the action of the play itself in order that the spectators might follow it intelligently. This introductory narrative runs up to seventy-six lines in the *Menaechmi,* to eighty-two in the *Rudens,* and to one hundred and fifty-two in the *Amphitruo*. In this way it becomes a short realistic story of every-day people, involving frequently a love intrigue, and told in the iambic senarius, the simplest form of verse. Following it is the more extended narrative of the comedy itself, with its incidents and dialogue. This combination of the condensed narrative in the story form, presented usually as a monologue in simple verse, and the expanded narrative in the dramatic form, with its conversational element, may well have suggested the writing of a realistic novel in prose. A slight, though not a fatal, objection to this theory lies in the fact that the prologues to comedy subsequent to Plautus changed in their character, and contain little narrative. This is not a serious objection, for the plays of Plautus were still known to the cultivated in the later period.

The mime gives us still more numerous points of contact with the work of Petronius than comedy does.[86] It is unfortunate, both for our understanding of Roman life and for our solution of the question before us, that only fragments of this form of dramatic composition have come down to us. Even from them, however, it is clear that the mime dealt with every-day life in a very frank, realistic way. The new comedy has its conventions in the matter of situations and language. The matron, for instance, must not be presented in a questionable light, and the language is the conversational speech of the better classes. The mime recognizes no such restrictions in its portrayal of life. The married woman, her stupid husband, and her lover are common figures in this form of the drama, and if we may draw an inference from the lately discovered fragments of Greek mimes, the speech was that of the common people. Again, the new comedy has its limited list of stock characters--the old man, the tricky slave, the parasite, and the others which we know so well in

Plautus and Terence, but as for the mime, any figure to be seen on the street may find a place in it--the rhetorician, the soldier, the legacy-hunter, the inn-keeper, or the town-crier. The doings of kings and heroes were parodied. We are even told that a comic Hector and Achilles were put on the stage, and the gods did not come off unscathed. All of these characteristic features of the mime remind us in a striking way of the novel of Petronius. His work, like the mime, is a realistic picture of low life which presents a great variety of characters and shows no regard for conventional morals. It is especially interesting to notice the element of parody, which we have already observed in Petronius, in both kinds of literary productions. The theory that Petronius may have had the composition of his *Satirae* suggested to him by plays of this type is greatly strengthened by the fact that the mime reached its highest point of popularity at the court in the time of Nero, in whose reign Petronius lived. In point of fact Petronius refers to the mime frequently. One of these passages is of peculiar significance in this connection. Encolpius and his comrades are entering the town of Croton and are considering what device they shall adopt so as to live without working. At last a happy idea occurs to Eumolpus, and he says: "Why don't we construct a mime?" and the mime is played, with Eumolpus as a fabulously rich man at the point of death, and the others as his attendants. The rôle makes a great hit, and all the vagabonds in the company play their assumed parts in their daily life at Croton with such skill that the legacy-hunters of the place load them with attentions and shower them with presents. This whole episode, in fact, may be thought of as a mime cast in the narrative form, and the same conception may be applied with great plausibility to the entire story of Encolpius.

We have thus far been attacking the question with which we are concerned from the side of the subject-matter and tone of the story of Petronius. Another method of approach is suggested by the Menippean satire,[87] the best specimens of which have come down to us in the fragments of Varro, one of Cicero's contemporaries. These satires are an *olla podrida,* dealing with all sorts of subjects in a satirical manner, sometimes put in the dialogue form and cast in a *mélange* of prose and verse. It is this last characteristic which is of special interest to us in this connection, because in the prose of Petronius verses are freely used. Sometimes, as we have observed above, they form an integral part of the narrative, and again they merely illustrate or expand a point touched on in the prose. If it were not aside from our immediate purpose it would be interesting to follow the history of this prose-poetical form from the time of Petronius on. After him it does not seem to have been used very much until the third and fourth centuries of our era. However, Martial in the first century prefixed a prose prologue to five books of his Epigrams, and one of these prologues ends with a poem of four lines. The several books of the *Silvae* of Statius are also preceded by prose letters of dedication. That strange imitation of the *Aulularia* of Plautus, of the fourth century, the *Querolus,* is in a form half prose and half verse. A sentence begins in prose and runs off into verse, as some of the epitaphs also do. The Epistles of Ausonius of the same century are compounded of prose and a great variety of verse. By the fifth and sixth centuries, a *mélange* of verse or a combination of prose and verse is very common, as one can see in the writings of Martianus Capella, Sidonius Apollinaris, Ennodius, and Boethius. It recurs again in modern times, for instance in Dante's *La Vita Nuova,* in Boccaccio, *Aucassin et Nicolette,* the *Heptameron,* the *Celtic Ballads,* the *Arabian Nights,* and in *Alice in Wonderland.*

A little thought suggests that the prose-poetic form is a natural medium of expression. A change from prose to verse, or from one form of verse to another, suggests a change in the emotional condition of a speaker or writer. We see that clearly enough illustrated in tragedy or comedy. In the thrilling scene in the *Captives of Plautus,* for example, where Tyndarus is in mortal terror lest the trick which he has played on his master, Hegio, may be discovered, and he be consigned to work in chains in the quarries, the verse is the trochaic septenarius. As soon as the suspense is over, it drops to the iambic senarius. If we should arrange the commoner Latin verses in a sequence according to the emotional effects which they produce, at the bottom of the series would stand the iambic senarius. Above that would come trochaic verse, and we should rise to higher planes of exaltation as we read the anapæstic, or cretic, or bacchiac. The greater part of life is commonplace. Consequently the common medium for conversation or for the narrative in a composition like comedy made up entirely of verse is the senarius. Now this form of verse in its simple, almost natural, quantitative arrangement is very close to prose, and it would be a short step to substitute prose for it as the basis of the story, interspersing verse here and there to secure variety, or when the emotions were called into play, just as lyric verses are interpolated in the iambic narrative. In this way the combination of different kinds of verse in the drama, and the prosimetrum of the Menippean satire and of Petronius, may be explained, and we see a possible line of descent from comedy and this form of satire to the *Satirae*.

These various theories of the origin of the romance of Petronius--that it may be related to the epic, to the serious heroic romance, to the bourgeois story of adventure developed out of the rhetorical exercise, to the Milesian tale, to the prologue of comedy, to the *verse-mélange* of comedy or the mime, or to the prose-poetical Menippean satire--are not, of necessity, it seems to me, mutually exclusive. His novel may well be thought of as a parody of the serious romance, with frequent reminiscences of the epic, a parody suggested to him by comedy and its prologue, by the mime, or by the short cynical Milesian tale, and cast in the form of the Menippean satire; or, so far as subject-matter and realistic treatment are concerned, the suggestion may have come directly from the mime, and if we can accept the theory of some scholars who have lately studied the mime, that it sometimes contained both prose and verse, we may be inclined to regard this type of literature as the immediate progenitor of the novel, even in the matter of external form, and leave the Menippean satire out of the line of descent. Whether the one or the other of these explanations of its origin recommends itself to us as probable, it is interesting to note, as we leave the subject, that, so far as our present information goes, the realistic romance seems to have been the invention of Petronius.

## Diocletian's Edict and the High Cost of Living

The history of the growth of paternalism in the Roman Empire is still to be written. It would be a fascinating and instructive record. In it the changes in the character of the Romans and in their social and economic conditions would come out clearly. It would disclose a strange mixture of worthy and unworthy motives in their statesmen and politicians, who were actuated sometimes by sympathy for the poor, sometimes by a desire for popular favor, by an honest wish to check extravagance or immorality, or by the fear that the discontent of the masses might drive them into revolution. We should find the Roman people, recognizing the menace to their simple, frugal way of living which lay in the inroads of Greek civilization, and turning in their helplessness to their officials, the censors, to protect them from a demoralization which, by their own efforts, they could not withstand. We should find the same officials preaching against race suicide, extravagant living, and evasion of public duties, and imposing penalties and restrictions in the most autocratic fashion on men of high and low degree alike who failed to adopt the official standards of conduct. We should read of laws enacted in the same spirit, laws restricting the number of guests that might be entertained on a single occasion, and prescribing penalties for guests and host alike, if the cost of a dinner exceeded the statutory limit. All this belongs to the early stage of paternal government. The motives were praiseworthy, even if the results were futile.

With the advent of the Gracchi, toward the close of the second century before our era, moral considerations become less noticeable, and paternalism takes on a more philanthropic and political character. We see this change reflected in the land laws and the corn laws. To take up first the free distribution of land by the state, in the early days of the Republic colonies of citizens were founded in the newly conquered districts of Italy to serve as garrisons on the frontier. It was a fair bargain between the citizen and the state. He received land, the state, protection. But with Tiberius Gracchus a change comes in. His colonists were to be settled in peaceful sections of Italy; they were to receive land solely because of their poverty. This was socialism or state philanthropy. Like the agrarian bill of Tiberius, the corn law of Gaius Gracchus, which provided for the sale of grain below the market price, was a paternal measure inspired in part by sympathy for the needy. The political element is clear in both cases also. The people who were thus favored by assignments of land and of food naturally supported the leaders who assisted them. Perhaps the extensive building of roads which Gaius Gracchus carried on should be mentioned in this connection. The ostensible purpose of these great highways, perhaps their primary purpose, was to develop Italy and to facilitate communication between different parts of the peninsula, but a large number of men was required for their construction, and Gaius Gracchus may well have taken the matter up, partly for the purpose of furnishing work to the unemployed. Out of these small beginnings developed the socialistic policy of later times. By the middle of the first century B.C., it is said that there were three hundred and twenty thousand persons receiving doles of corn from the state, and, if the people could look to the government for the necessities of life, why might they not hope to have it supply their less pressing needs? Or, to put it in another way, if one politician won their support by giving them corn, why might not another increase his popularity by providing them with amusement and with the comforts of life? Presents of oil and clothing naturally follow, the giving of games and theatrical performances at the expense of the state, and the building of porticos and public baths. As the government and wealthy citizens assumed a larger measure of responsibility for the welfare of the citizens, the people became more and more dependent upon them and less capable of managing their own affairs. An indication of this change we see in the decline of local self-government and the assumption by the central administration of responsibility for the conduct of public business in the towns of Italy. This last consideration suggests another phase of Roman history which a study of paternalism would bring out--I mean the effect of its introduction on the character of the Roman people.

The history of paternalism in Rome, when it is written, might approach the subject from several different points. If the writer were inclined to interpret history on the economic side, he might find the explanation of the change in the policy of the government toward its citizens in the introduction of slave labor which, under the Republic, drove the free laborer to the wall and made him look to the state for help, in the decline of agriculture, and the growth of capitalism. The sociologist would notice the drift of the people toward the cities and the sudden massing there of large numbers of persons who could not provide for themselves and in their discontent might overturn society. The historian who concerns himself with political changes mainly, would notice the socialistic legislation of the Gracchi and their political successors and would connect the growth of paternalism with the development of democracy. In all these explanations there would be a certain measure of truth.

But I am not planning here to write a history of paternalism among the Romans. That is one of the projects which I had been reserving for the day when the Carnegie Foundation should present me with a wooden sword and allow me to retire from the arena of academic life. But, alas! the trustees of that beneficent institution, by the revision which they have lately made of the conditions under which a university professor may withdraw from active service, have in their wisdom put off that day of academic leisure to the Greek Kalends, and my dream vanishes into the distance with it.

Here I wish to present only an episode in this history which we have been discussing, an episode which is unique, however, in ancient and, so far as I know, in modern history. Our knowledge of the incident comes from an edict of the Emperor Diocletian, and this document has a direct bearing on a subject of present-day discussion, because it contains a diatribe against the high cost of living and records the heroic attempt which the Roman government made to reduce it. In his effort to bring prices down to what he considered a normal level, Diocletian did not content himself with such half-measures as we are trying in our attempts to suppress combinations in restraint of trade, but he boldly fixed the maximum prices at which beef, grain, eggs, clothing, and other articles could be sold, and prescribed the penalty of death for any one who disposed of his wares at a higher figure. His edict is a very comprehensive document, and specifies prices for seven hundred or eight hundred different articles. This systematic attempt to regulate trade was very much in keeping with the character of Diocletian and his theory of government. Perhaps no Roman emperor, with the possible exception of Hadrian, showed such extraordinary administrative ability and proposed so many sweeping social reforms as Diocletian did. His systematic attempt to suppress Christianity is a case in point, and in the last twenty years of his reign he completely reorganized the government. He frankly introduced the monarchical principle, fixed upon a method of succession to the throne, redivided the provinces, established a carefully graded system of officials, concerned himself with court etiquette and dress, and reorganized the coinage and the system of taxation. We are not surprised therefore that he had the courage to attack this difficult question of high prices, and that his plan covered almost all the articles which his subjects would have occasion to buy.

It is almost exactly two centuries since the first fragments of the edict dealing with the subject were brought to light. They were discovered in Caria, in 1709, by William Sherard, the English consul at Smyrna. Since then, from time to time, other fragments of tablets containing parts of the edict have been found in Egypt, Asia Minor, and Greece. At present portions of twenty-nine copies of it are known. Fourteen of them are in Latin and fifteen in Greek. The Greek versions differ from one another, while the Latin texts are identical, except for the stone-cutters' mistakes here and there. These facts make it clear that the original document was in Latin, and was translated into Greek by the local officials of each town where the tablets were set up. We have already noticed that specimens of the edict have not been found outside of Egypt, Greece, and Asia Minor, and this was the part of the Roman world where Diocletian ruled. Scholars have also observed that almost all the manufactured articles which are mentioned come from Eastern points. From these facts it has been inferred that the edict was to apply to the East only, or perhaps more probably that Diocletian drew it up for his part of the Roman world, and that before it could be applied to the West it was repealed.

From the pieces which were then known, a very satisfactory reconstruction of the document was made by Mommsen and published in the *Corpus of Latin Inscriptions*.[88]

The work of restoration was like putting together the parts of a picture puzzle where some of the pieces are lacking. Fragments are still coming to light, and possibly we may have the complete text some day. As it is, the introduction is complete, and perhaps four-fifths of the list of articles with prices attached are extant. The introduction opens with a stately list of the titles of the two Augusti and the two Cæsars, which fixes the date of the proclamation as 301 A.D. Then follows a long recital of the circumstances which have led the government to adopt this drastic method of controlling prices. This introduction is one of the most extraordinary pieces of bombast, mixed metaphors, loose syntax, and incoherent expressions that Latin literature possesses. One is tempted to infer from its style that it was the product of Diocletian's own pen. He was a man of humble origin, and would not live in Rome for fear of being laughed at on account of his plebeian training. The florid and awkward style of these introductory pages is exactly what we should expect from a man of such antecedents.

It is very difficult to translate them into intelligible English, but some conception of their style and contents may be had from one or two extracts. In explaining the situation which confronts the world, the Emperor writes: "For, if the raging avarice ... which, without regard for mankind, increases and develops by leaps and bounds, we will not say from year to year, month to month, or day to day, but almost from hour to hour, and even from minute to minute, could be held in check by some regard for moderation, or if the welfare of the people could calmly tolerate this mad license from which, in a situation like this, it suffers in the worst possible fashion from day to day, some ground would appear, perhaps, for concealing the truth and saying nothing; ... but inasmuch as there is only seen a mad desire without control, to pay no heed to the needs of the many, ... it seems good to us, as we look into the future, to us who are the fathers of the people, that justice intervene to settle matters impartially, in order that that which, long hoped for, humanity itself could not bring about may be secured for the common government of all by the remedies which our care affords.... Who is of so hardened a heart and so untouched by a feeling for humanity that he can be unaware, nay that he has not noticed, that in the sale of wares which are exchanged in the market, or dealt with in the daily business of the cities, an exorbitant tendency in prices has spread to such an extent that the unbridled desire of plundering is held in check neither by abundance nor by seasons of plenty!"

If we did not know that this was found on tablets sixteen centuries old, we might think that we were reading a newspaper diatribe against the cold-storage plant or the beef trust. What the Emperor has decided to do to remedy the situation he sets forth toward the end of the introduction. He says: "It is our pleasure, therefore, that those prices which the subjoined written summary specifies, be held in observance throughout all our domain, that all may know that license to go above the same has been cut off.... It is our pleasure (also) that if any man shall have boldly come into conflict with this formal statute, he shall put his life in peril.... In the same peril also shall he be placed who, drawn along by avarice in his desire to buy, shall have conspired against these statutes. Nor shall he be esteemed innocent of the same crime who, having articles necessary for daily life and use, shall have decided hereafter that they can be held back, since the punishment ought to be even heavier for him who causes need than for him who violates the laws."

The lists which follow are arranged in three columns which give respectively the article, the unit of measure, and the price.[89]

Frumenti K¯M¯ Hordei K¯M¯ unum ?? c(entum) Centenum sive sicale " " " ?? sexa(ginta) Mili pisti " " " ?? centu(m) Mili integri " " ?? quinquaginta'

The first item (frumentum) is wheat, which is sold by the K¯M¯ (kastrensis modius=18½ quarts), but the price is lacking. Barley is sold by the kastrensis modius at ?? centum (centum denarii = 43 cents) and so on.

Usually a price list is not of engrossing interest, but the tables of Diocletian furnish us a picture of material conditions throughout the Empire in his time which cannot be had from any other source, and for that reason deserve some attention. This consideration emboldens me to set down some extracts in the following pages from the body of the edict:

## Extracts from Diocletian's List of Maximum Prices

### I

In the tables given here the Latin and Greek names of the articles listed have been turned into English. The present-day accepted measure of quantity--for instance, the bushel or the quart--has been substituted for the ancient unit, and the corresponding price for the modern unit of measure is given. Thus barley was to be sold by the kastrensis modius (=18½ quarts) at 100 denarii (=43.5 cents). At this rate a bushel of barley would have brought 74.5 cents. For convenience in reference the numbers of the chapters and of the items adopted in the text of Mommsen are used here. Only selected articles are given.

(Unit of Measure, the Bushel)

| | |
|---|---|
| 1 Wheat | |
| 2 Barley | 74.5 cents |
| 3 Rye | 45 " |
| 4 Millet, ground | 74.5 " |
| 6 Millet, whole | 37 " |
| 7 Spelt, hulled | 74.5 " |
| 8 Spelt, not hulled | 22.5 " |
| 9 Beans, ground | 74.5 " |
| 10 Beans, not ground | 45 " |
| 11 Lentils | 74.5 " |
| 12-16 Peas, various sorts | 45-74.5 " |
| 17 Oats | 22.5 " |
| 31 Poppy seeds | $1.12 |
| 34 Mustard | $1.12 |
| 35 Prepared mustard, quart | 6 " |

### II

(Unit of Measure, the Quart)

| | |
|---|---|
| 1a Wine from Picenum | 22.5 cents |
| 2 Wine from Tibur | 22.5 " |
| 7 Wine from Falernum | 22.5 " |
| 10 Wine of the country | 6 " |
| 11-12 Beer | 1.5-3 " |

III

(Unit of Measure, the Quart)

| | |
|---|---|
| 1a Oil, first quality | 30.3 cents |
| 2 Oil, second quality | 18 " |
| 5 Vinegar | 4.3 " |
| 8 Salt, bushel | 74.5 " |
| 10 Honey, best | 30.3 " |
| 11 Honey, second quality | 15 " |

IV

(Unit, Unless Otherwise Noted, Pound Avoirdupois)

| | |
|---|---|
| 1a Pork | 7.3 cents |
| 2 Beef | 4.9 " |
| 3 Goat's flesh or mutton | 4.9 " |
| 6 Pig's liver | 9.8 " |
| 8 Ham, best | 12 " |
| 21 Goose, artificially fed (1) | 87 " |
| 22 Goose, not artificially fed (1) | 43.5 " |
| 23 Pair of fowls | 36 " |
| 29 Pair of pigeons | 10.5 " |
| 47 Lamb | 7.3 " |
| 48 Kid | 7.3 " |
| 50 Butter | 9.8 " |

V

(Unit, the Pound)

| | |
|---|---|
| 1a Sea fish with sharp spines | 14.6 cents |
| 2 Fish, second quality | 9.7 " |
| 3 River fish, best quality | 7.3 " |
| 4 Fish, second quality | 4.8 " |
| 5 Salt fish | 8.3 " |
| 6 Oysters (by the hundred) | 43.5 " |
| 11 Dry cheese | 7.3 " |
| 12 Sardines | 9.7 " |

VI

| | |
|---|---|
| 1 Artichokes, large (5) | 4.3 cents |
| 7 Lettuce, best (5) | 1.7 " |
| 9 Cabbages, best (5) | 1.7 " |
| 10 Cabbages, small (10) | 1.7 " |
| 18 Turnips, large (10) | 1.7 " |
| 24 Watercress, per bunch of 20 | 4.3 " |
| 28 Cucumbers, first quality (10) | 1.7 " |
| 29 Cucumbers, small (20) | 1.7 " |
| 34 Garden asparagus, per bunch (25) | 2.6 " |
| 35 Wild asparagus (50) | 1.7 " |
| 38 Shelled green beans, quart | 3 " |
| 43 Eggs (4) | 1.7 " |
| 46 Snails, large (20) | 1.7 " |
| 65 Apples, best (10) | 1.7 " |
| 67 Apples, small (40) | 1.7 " |
| 78 Figs, best (25) | 1.7 " |
| 80 Table grapes (2.8 pound) | 1.7 " |
| 95 Sheep's milk, quart | 6 " |
| 96 Cheese, fresh, quart | 6 " |

VII

(Where (k) Is Set Down the Workman Receives His "Keep" Also)

| | |
|---|---|
| 1a Manual laborer (k) | 10.8 cents |
| 2 Bricklayer (k) | 21.6 " |
| 3 Joiner (interior work) (k) | 21.6 " |
| 3a Carpenter (k) | 21.6 " |
| 4 Lime-burner (k) | 21.6 " |
| 5 Marble-worker (k) | 26 " |
| 6 Mosaic-worker (fine work) (k) | 26 " |
| 7 Stone-mason (k) | 21.6 " |
| 8 Wall-painter (k) | 32.4 " |
| 9 Figure-painter (k) | 64.8 " |
| 10 Wagon-maker (k) | 21.6 " |
| 11 Smith (k) | 21.6 " |
| 12 Baker (k) | 21.6 " |
| 13 Ship-builder, for sea-going ships (k) | 26 " |
| 14 Ship-builder, for river boats (k) | 21.6 " |
| 17 Driver, for camel, ass, or mule (k) | 10.8 " |

| | |
|---|---|
| 18 Shepherd (k) | 8.7 " |
| 20 Veterinary, for cutting, and straightening hoofs, per animal | 2.6 " |
| 22 Barber, for each man | .9 cent |
| 23 Sheep-shearer, for each sheep (k) | .9 " |
| 24a Coppersmith, for work in brass, per pound | 3.5 cents |
| 25 Coppersmith, for work in copper, per pound | 2.6 " |
| 26 Coppersmith for finishing vessels, per pound | 2.6 " |
| 27 Coppersmith, for finishing figures and statues, per pound | 1.7 " |
| 29 Maker of statues, etc., per day (k) | 32.4 " |
| 31 Water-carrier, per day (k) | 10.9 " |
| 32 Sewer-cleaner, per day (k) | 10.9 " |
| 33 Knife-grinder, for old sabre | 10.9 " |
| 36 Knife-grinder, for double axe | 3.5 " |
| 39 Writer, 100 lines best writing | 10.9 " |
| 40 Writer, 100 lines ordinary writing | 8.7 " |
| 41 Document writer for record of 100 lines | 4.3 " |
| 42 Tailor, for cutting out and finishing overgarment of first | 26.1 " |
| 43 Tailor, for cutting out and finishing overgarment of second | 17.4 " |
| 44 For a large cowl | 10.9 " |
| 45 For a small cowl | 8.7 " |
| 46 For trousers | 8.7 " |
| 52 Felt horse-blanket, black or white, 3 pounds weight | 43.5 " |
| 53 Cover, first quality, with embroidery, 3 pounds weight | $1.09 |
| 64 Gymnastic teacher, per pupil, per month | 21.6 cents |
| 65 Employee to watch children, per child, per month | 21.6 " |
| 66 Elementary teacher, per pupil, per month | 21.6 " |
| 67 Teacher of arithmetic, per pupil, per month | 32.6 " |
| 68 Teacher of stenography, per pupil, per month | 32.6 " |
| 69 Writing-teacher, per pupil, per month | 21.6 " |
| 70 Teacher of Greek, Latin, geometry, per pupil, per month | 87 " |
| 71 Teacher of rhetoric, per pupil, per month | $1.09 |
| 72 Advocate or counsel for presenting a case | $1.09 |
| 73 For finishing a case | $4.35 |
| 74 Teacher of architecture, per pupil, per month | 43.5 cents |
| 75 Watcher of clothes in public bath, | |

for each patron .9 cent

## VIII

| | |
|---|---|
| 1a Hide, Babylonian, first quality | $2.17 |
| 2 Hide, Babylonian, second quality | $1.74 |
| 4 Hide, Phœnician (?) | 43 cents |
| 6a Cowhide, unworked, first quality | $2.17 |
| 7 Cowhide, prepared for shoe soles | $3.26 |
| 9 Hide, second quality, unworked | $1.31 |
| 10 Hide, second quality, worked | $2.17 |
| 11 Goatskin, large, unworked | 17 cents |
| 12 Goatskin, large, worked | 22 " |
| 13 Sheepskin, large, unworked | 8.7 " |
| 14 Sheepskin, large, worked | 18 " |
| 17 Kidskin, unworked | 4.3 " |
| 18 Kidskin, worked | 7 " |
| 27 Wolfskin, unworked | 10.8 " |
| 28 Wolfskin, worked | 17.4 " |
| 33 Bearskin, large, unworked | 43 " |
| 39 Leopardskin, unworked | $4.35 |
| 41 Lionskin, worked | $4.35 |

## IX

| | |
|---|---|
| 5a Boots, first quality, for mule-drivers and peasants, per pair, without nails | 52 cents |
| 6 Soldiers' boots, without nails " | |
| 7 Patricians' shoes " | |
| 8 Senatorial shoes " | |
| 9 Knights' shoes | 30.5 " |
| 10 Women's boots | 26 " |
| 11 Soldiers' shoes | 32.6 " |
| 15 Cowhide shoes for women, double soles | 21.7 " |
| 16 Cowhide shoes for women, single soles | 13 " |
| 20 Men's slippers | 26 " |
| 21 Women's slippers | 21.7 " |

## XVI

| | |
|---|---|
| 8a Sewing-needle, finest quality | 1.7 cents |
| 9 Sewing-needle, second quality | .9 cent |

## XVII

| | |
|---|---|
| 1 Transportation, 1 person, 1 mile | .9 cent |
| 2 Rent for wagon, 1 mile | 5 cents |
| 3 Freight charges for wagon containing up to 1,200 pounds, per mile | 8.7 " |
| 4 Freight charges for camel load of 600 pounds, per mile | 3.5 " |
| 5 Rent for laden ass, per mile | 1.8 " |
| 7 Hay and straw, 3 pounds | .9 cent |

## XVIII

| | |
|---|---|
| 1a Goose-quills, per pound | 43.5 cents |
| 11a Ink, per pound | 5 " |
| 12 Reed pens from Paphos (10) | 1.7 " |
| 13 Reed pens, second quality (20) | 1.7 " |

## XIX

| | |
|---|---|
| 1 Military mantle, finest quality | $17.40 |
| 2 Undergarment, fine | $8.70 |
| 3 Undergarment, ordinary | $5.44 |
| 5 White bed blanket, finest sort, 12 pounds weight | $6.96 |
| 7 Ordinary cover, 10 pounds weight | $2.18 |
| 28 Laodicean Dalmatica [i.e., a tunic with sleeves] | $8.70 |
| 36 British mantle, with cowl | $26.08 |
| 39 Numidian mantle, with cowl | $13.04 |
| 42 African mantle, with cowl | $6.52 |
| 51 Laodicean storm coat, finest quality | $21.76 |
| 60 Gallic soldier's cloak | $43.78 |
| 61 African soldier's cloak | $2.17 |

XX

| | |
|---|---|
| 1a For an embroiderer, for embroidering a half-silk undergarment, per ounce | 87 cents |
| 5 For a gold embroiderer, if he work in gold, for finest work, per ounce | $4.35 |
| 9 For a silk weaver, who works on stuff half-silk, besides "keep," per day | 11 cents |

XXI

| | |
|---|---|
| 2 For working Tarentine or Laodicean or other foreign wool, with keep, per pound | 13 cents |
| 5 A linen weaver for fine work, with keep, per day | 18 " |

XXII

| | |
|---|---|
| 4 Fuller's charges for a cloak or mantle, new | 13 cents |
| 6 Fuller's charges for a woman's coarse Dalmatica, new | 21.7 " |
| 9 Fuller's charges for a new half-silk undergarment | 76 " |
| 22 Fuller's charges for a new Laodicean mantle. | 76 " |

XXIII

| | |
|---|---|
| 1 White silk, per pound | $52.22 |

XXIV

| | |
|---|---|
| 1 Genuine purple silk, per pound | $652.20 |
| 2 Genuine purple wool, per pound | $217.40 |
| 3 Genuine light purple wool, per pound | $139.26 |
| 8 Nicæan scarlet wool, per pound | $6.53 |

XXV

| | |
|---|---|
| 1 Washed Tarentine wool, per pound | 76 cents |
| 2 Washed Laodicean wool, per pound | 65 " |
| 3 Washed wool from Asturia, per pound | 43.5 " |
| 4 Washed wool, best medium quality, per pound | 21.7 " |
| 5 All other washed wools, per pound | 10.8 " |

XXVI

| | |
|---|---|
| 7a Coarse linen thread, first quality, per pound | $3.13 |
| 8 Coarse linen thread, second quality, per pound | $2.61 |
| 9 Coarse linen thread, third quality, per pound | $1.96 |

XXX

| | |
|---|---|
| 1 Pure gold in bars or in coined pieces, per pound | 50,000 denarii |
| 3 Artificers, working in metal, per pound | $21.76 |
| 4 Gold-beaters, per pound | $13.06 |

Throughout the lists, as one may see, articles are grouped in a systematic way. First we find grain and vegetables; then wine, oil, vinegar, salt, honey, meat, fish, cheese, salads, and nuts. After these articles, in chapter VII, we pass rather unexpectedly to the wages of the field laborer, the carpenter, the painter, and of other skilled and unskilled workmen. Then follow leather, shoes, saddles, and other kinds of raw material and manufactured wares until we reach a total of more than eight hundred articles. As we have said, the classification is in the main systematic, but there are some strange deviations from a systematic arrangement. Eggs, for instance, are in table VI with salads, vegetables, and fruits. Bücher, who has discussed some phases of this price list, has acutely surmised that perhaps the tables in whole, or in part, were drawn up by the directors of imperial factories and magazines. The government levied tribute "in kind," and it must have provided depots throughout the provinces for the reception of contributions from its subjects. Consequently in making out these tables it would very likely call upon the directors of these magazines for assistance, and each of them in making his report would naturally follow to some extent the list of articles which the imperial depot controlled by him, carried in stock. At all events, we see evidence of an expert hand in the list of linens, which includes one hundred and thirty-nine articles of different qualities.

As we have noticed in the passage quoted from the introduction, it is unlawful for a person to charge more for any of his wares than the amount specified in the law. Consequently, the prices are not normal, but maximum prices. However, since the imperial lawgivers evidently believed that the necessities of life were being sold at exorbitant rates, the maximum which they fixed was very likely no greater than the prevailing market price. Here and there, as in the nineteenth chapter of the document, the text is given in tablets from two or more places. In such cases the prices are the same, so that apparently no allowance was made for the cost of carriage, although with some articles, like oysters and sea-fish, this item must have had an appreciable value, and it certainly should have been taken into account in fixing the prices of "British mantles" or "Gallic soldiers' cloaks" of chapter XIX. The quantities for which prices are given are so small--a pint of wine, a pair of fowls, twenty snails, ten apples, a bunch of asparagus--that evidently Diocletian had the "ultimate consumer" in mind, and fixed the retail price in his edict. This is fortunate for us, because it helps us to get at the cost of living in the early part of the fourth century. There is good reason for believing that the system of barter prevailed much more generally at that time than it does to-day. Probably the farmer often exchanged his grain, vegetables, and eggs for shoes and cloth, without receiving or paying out money, so that the money prices fixed for his products would not affect him in every transaction as they would affect the present-day farmer. The unit of money which is used throughout the edict is the copper denarius, and fortunately the value of a pound of fine gold is given as 50,000 denarii. This fixes the value of the denarius as .4352 cent, or approximately four-tenths of a cent. It is implied in the introduction that the purpose of the law is to protect the people, and especially the soldiers, from extortion, but possibly, as Bücher has surmised, the emperor may have wished to maintain or to raise the value of the denarius, which had been steadily declining because of the addition of alloy to the coin. If this was the emperor's object, possibly the value of the denarius is set somewhat too high, but it probably does not materially exceed its exchange value, and in any case, the relative values of articles given in the tables are not affected.

The tables bring out a number of points of passing interest. From chapter II it seems to follow that Italian wines retained their ancient pre-eminence, even in the fourth century. They alone are quoted among the foreign wines. Table VI gives us a picture of the village market. On market days the farmer brings his artichokes, lettuce, cabbages, turnips, and other fresh vegetables into the market town and exposes them for sale in the public square, as the country people in Italy do to-day. The seventh chapter, in which wages are given, is perhaps of liveliest interest. In this connection we should bear in mind the fact that slavery existed in the Roman Empire, that owners of slaves trained them to various occupations and hired them out by the day or job, and that, consequently the prices paid for slave labor fixed the scale of wages. However, there was a steady decline under the Empire in the number of slaves, and competition with them in the fourth century did not materially affect the wages of the free laborer. It is interesting, in this chapter, to notice that the teacher and the advocate (Nos. 66-73) are classed with the carpenter and tailor. It is a pleasant passing reflection for the teacher of Greek and Latin to find that his predecessors were near the top of their profession, if we may draw this inference from their remuneration when compared with that of other teachers. It is worth observing also that the close association between the classics and mathematics, and their acceptance as the corner-stone of the higher training, to which we have been accustomed for centuries, seems to be recognized (VII, 70) even at this early date. We expect to find the physician mentioned with the teacher and advocate, but probably it was too much even for Diocletian's skill, in reducing things to a system, to estimate the comparative value of a physician's services in a case of measles and typhoid fever.

The bricklayer, the joiner, and the carpenter (VII, 2-3a), inasmuch as they work on the premises of their employer, receive their "keep" as well as a fixed wage, while the knife-grinder and the tailor (VII, 33, 42) work in their own shops, and naturally have their meals at home. The silk-weaver (XX, 9) and the linen-weaver (XXI, 5) have their "keep" also, which seems to indicate that private houses had their own looms, which is quite in harmony with the practices of our fathers. The carpenter and joiner are paid by the day, the teacher by the month, the knife-grinder, the tailor, the barber (VII, 22) by the piece, and the coppersmith (VII, 24a-27) according to the amount of metal which he uses. Whether the difference between the prices of shoes for the patrician, the senator, and the knight (IX, 7-9) represents a difference in the cost of making the three kinds, or is a tax put on the different orders of nobility, cannot be determined. The high prices set on silk and wool dyed with purple (XXIV) correspond to the pre-eminent position of that imperial color in ancient times.

The tables which the edict contains call our attention to certain striking differences between ancient and modern industrial and economic conditions. Of course the list of wage-earners is incomplete. The inscriptions which the trades guilds have left us record many occupations which are not mentioned here, but in them and in these lists we miss any reference to large groups of men who hold a prominent place in our modern industrial reports--I mean men working in printing-offices, factories, foundries, and machine-shops, and employed by transportation companies. Nothing in the document suggests the application of power to the manufacture of articles, the assembling of men in a common workshop, or the use of any other machine than the hand loom and the mill for the grinding of corn. In the way of articles offered for sale, we miss certain items which find a place in every price-list of household necessities, such articles as sugar, molasses, potatoes, cotton cloth, tobacco, coffee, and tea. The list of stimulants (II) is, in fact, very brief, including as it does only a few kinds of wine and beer.

At the present moment, when the high cost of living is a subject which engages the attention of the economist, politician, and householder, as it did that of Diocletian and his contemporaries, the curious reader will wish to know how wages and the prices of food in 301 A.D. compare with those of to-day. In the two tables which follow, such a comparison is attempted for some of the more important articles and occupations.

### Articles of Food

| | Price in 301 A.D. | Price in 1906 A.D. |
|---|---|---|
| Wheat, per bushel | 33.6 cents | $1.19 |
| Rye, per bushel | 45 " | 79 cents |
| Beans, per bushel | 45 " | $3.20 |
| Barley, per bushel | 74.5 " | 55 cents |
| Vinegar, per quart | 4.3 " | 5-7 " |
| Fresh pork, per pound | 7.3 " | 14-16 " |
| Beef, per pound | 4.9 " | { 9-12 "<br>{15-18 " |
| Mutton, per pound | 4.9 " | 13-16 " |
| Ham, per pound | 12 " | 18-25 " |
| Fowls, per pair | 26 " | |
| Fowls, per pound | | 14-18 " |
| Butter, per pound | 9.8 " | 26-32 " |
| Fish, river, fresh, per pound | 7.3 " | 12-15 " |
| Fish, sea, fresh, per pound | 9-14 " | 8-14 cents |
| Fish, salt, per pound | 8.3 " | 8-15 " |
| Cheese, per pound | 7.3 " | 17-20 " |
| Eggs, per dozen | 5.1 " | 25-30 " |
| Milk, cow's, per quart | | 6-8 " |
| Milk, sheep's, per quart | 6 " | |

### Wages Per Day

| | | |
|---|---|---|
| Unskilled workman | 10.8 cents (k) | $1.20-2.24 |
| Bricklayer | 21.6 " (k) | 4.50-6.50 |
| Carpenter | 21.6 " (k) | 2.50-4.00 |
| Stone-mason | 21.6 " (k) | 3.70-4.90 |
| Painter | 32.4 " (k) | 2.75-4.00 |
| Blacksmith | 21.6 " (k) | 2.15-3.20 |
| Ship-builder | 21-26 " (k) | 2.15-3.50 |

We are not so much concerned in knowing the prices of meat, fish, eggs, and flour in 301 and 1911 A.D. as we are in finding out whether the Roman or the American workman could buy more of these commodities with the returns for his labor. A starting point for such an estimate is furnished by the Eighteenth Annual Report of the Commissioner of Labor, on the "Cost of Living and Retail Prices of Food" (1903), and by Bulletin No. 77 of the Bureau of Labor (1908). In the first of these documents (pp. 582, 583) the expenditure for rent, fuel, food, and other necessities of life in 11,156 normal American families whose incomes range from $200 to $1,200 per year is given. In the other report (p. 344 *f.*) similar statistics are given for 1,944 English urban families. In the first case the average amount spent per year was $617, of which $266, or a little less than a half of the entire income, was used in the purchase of food. The statistics for England show a somewhat larger relative amount spent for food. Almost exactly one-third of this expenditure for the normal American family was for meat and fish.[94] Now, if we take the wages of the Roman carpenter, for instance, as 21 cents per day, and add one-fourth or one-third for his "keep," those of the same American workman as $2.50 to $4.00, it is clear that the former received only a ninth or a fifteenth as much as the latter, while the average price of pork, beef, mutton, and ham (7.3 cents) in 301 A.D. was about a third of the average (19.6 cents) of the same articles to-day. The relative averages of wheat, rye, and barley make a still worse showing for ancient times while fresh fish was nearly as high in Diocletian's time as it is in our own day. The ancient and modern prices of butter and eggs stand at the ratio of one to three and one to six respectively. For the urban workman, then, in the fourth century, conditions of life must have been almost intolerable, and it is hard to understand how he managed to keep soul and body together, when almost all the nutritious articles of food were beyond his means. The taste of meat, fish, butter, and eggs must have been almost unknown to him, and probably even the coarse bread and vegetables on which he lived were limited in amount. The peasant proprietor who could raise his own cattle and grain would not find the burden so hard to bear.

Only one question remains for us to answer. Did Diocletian succeed in his bold attempt to reduce the cost of living? Fortunately the answer is given us by Lactantius in the book which he wrote in 313-314 A.D., "On the Deaths of Those Who Persecuted (the Christians)." The title of Lactantius's work would not lead us to expect a very sympathetic treatment of Diocletian, the arch-persecutor, but his account of the actual outcome of the incident is hardly open to question. In Chapter VII of his treatise, after setting forth the iniquities of the Emperor in constantly imposing new burdens on the people, he writes: "And when he had brought on a state of exceeding high prices by his different acts of injustice, he tried to fix by law the prices of articles offered for sale. Thereupon, for the veriest trifles much blood was shed, and out of fear nothing was offered for sale, and the scarcity grew much worse, until, after the death of many persons, the law was repealed from mere necessity." Thus came to an end this early effort to reduce the high cost of living. Sixty years later the Emperor Julian made a similar attempt on a small scale. He fixed the price of corn for the people of Antioch by an edict. The holders of grain hoarded their stock. The Emperor brought supplies of it into the city from Egypt and elsewhere and sold it at the legal price. It was bought up by speculators, and in the end Julian, like Diocletian, had to acknowledge his inability to cope with an economic law.

## Private Benefactions and Their Effect on the Municipal Life of the Romans

In the early days the authority of the Roman father over his wife, his sons, and his daughters was absolute. He did what seemed to him good for his children. His oversight and care extended to all the affairs of their lives. The state was modelled on the family and took over the autocratic power of the paterfamilias. It is natural to think of it, therefore, as a paternal government, and the readiness with which the Roman subordinated his own will and sacrificed his personal interests to those of the community seems to show his acceptance of this theory of his relation to the government. But this conception is correct in part only. A paternal government seeks to foster all the common interests of its people and to provide for their common needs. This the Roman state did not try to do, and if we think of it as a paternal government, in the ordinary meaning of that term, we lose sight of the partnership between state supervision and individual enterprise in ministering to the common needs and desires, which was one of the marked features of Roman life. In fact, the gratification of the individual citizen's desire for those things which he could not secure for himself depended in the Roman Empire, as it depends in this country, not solely on state support, but in part on state aid, and in part on private generosity. We see the truth of this very clearly in studying the history of the Roman city. The phase of Roman life which we have just noted may not fit into the ideas of Roman society which we have hitherto held, but we can understand it as no other people can, because in the United States and in England we are accustomed to the co-operation of private initiative and state action in the establishment and maintenance of universities, libraries, museums, and all sorts of charitable institutions.

If we look at the growth of private munificence under the Republic, we shall see that citizens showed their generosity particularly in the construction of public buildings, partly or entirely at their own expense. In this way some of the basilicas in Rome and elsewhere which served as courts of justice and halls of exchange were constructed. The great Basilica Æmilia, for instance, whose remains may be seen in the Forum to-day, was constructed by an Æmilius in the second century before our era, and was accepted as a charge by his descendants to be kept in condition and improved at the expense of the Æmilian family. Under somewhat similar conditions Pompey built the great theatre which bore his name, the first permanent theatre to be built in Rome, and always considered one of the wonders of the city. The cost of this structure was probably covered by the treasure which he brought back from his campaigns in the East. In using the spoils of a successful war to construct buildings or memorials in Rome, he was following the example of Mummius, the conqueror of Corinth, and other great generals who had preceded him. The purely philanthropic motive does not bulk largely in these gifts to the citizens, because the people whose armies had won the victories were part owners at least of the spoils, and because the victorious leader who built the structure was actuated more by the hope of transmitting the memory of his achievements to posterity in some conspicuous and imperishable monument than by a desire to benefit his fellow citizens.

These two motives, the one egoistic and the other altruistic, actuated all the Roman emperors in varying degrees. The activity of Augustus in such matters comes out clearly in the record of his reign, which he has left us in his own words. This remarkable bit of autobiography, known as the "Deeds of the Deified Augustus," the Emperor had engraved on bronze tablets, placed in front of his mausoleum. The original has disappeared, but fortunately a copy of it has been found on the walls of a ruined temple at Ancyra, in Asia Minor, and furnishes us abundant proof of the great improvements which he made in the city of Rome. We are told in it that from booty he paid for the construction of the Forum of Augustus, which was some four hundred feet long, three hundred wide, and was surrounded by a wall one hundred and twenty feet high, covered on the inside with marble and stucco. Enclosed within it and built with funds coming from the same source was the magnificent temple of Mars the Avenger, which had as its principal trophies the Roman standards recovered from the Parthians. This forum and temple are only two items in the long list of public improvements which Augustus records in his imperial epitaph, for, as he proudly writes: "In my sixth consulship, acting under a decree of the senate, I restored eighty-two temples in the city, neglecting no temple which needed repair at the time." Besides the temples, he mentions a large number of theatres, porticos, basilicas, aqueducts, roads, and bridges which he built in Rome or in Italy outside the city.

But the Roman people had come to look for acts of generosity from their political as well as from their military leaders, and this factor, too, must be taken into account in the case of Augustus. In the closing years of the Republic, candidates for office and men elected to office saw that one of the most effective ways of winning and holding their popularity was to give public entertainments, and they vied with one another in the costliness of the games and pageants which they gave the people. The well-known case of Cæsar will be recalled, who, during his term as ædile, or commissioner of public works, bankrupted himself by his lavish expenditures on public improvements, and on the games, in which he introduced three hundred and twenty pairs of gladiators for the amusement of the people. In his book, "On the Offices," Cicero tells us of a thrifty rich man, named Mamercus, who aspired to public office, but avoided taking the ædileship, which stood in the regular sequence of minor offices, in order that he might escape the heavy outlay for public entertainment expected of the ædile. As a consequence, when later he came up for the consulship, the people punished him by defeating him at the polls. To check the growth of these methods of securing votes, Cicero, in his consulship, brought in a corrupt practices act, which forbade citizens to give gladiatorial exhibitions within two years of any election in which they were candidates. We may doubt if this measure was effective. The Roman was as clever as the American politician in accomplishing his purpose without going outside the law. Perhaps an incident in the life of Cicero's young friend, Curio, is a case in point. It was an old Roman custom to celebrate the ninth day after a burial as a solemn family festival, and some time in the second century before our era the practice grew up of giving gladiatorial contests on these occasions. The versatile Curio, following this practice, testified his respect for his father's memory by giving the people such elaborate games that he never escaped from the financial difficulties in which they involved him. However, this tribute of pious affection greatly enhanced his popularity, and perhaps did not expose him to the rigors of Cicero's law.

These gifts from generals, from distinguished citizens, and from candidates for office do not go far to prove a generous or philanthropic spirit on the part of the donors, but they show clearly enough that the practice of giving large sums of money to embellish the city, and to please the public, had grown up under the Republic, and that the people of Rome had come to regard it as the duty of their distinguished fellow citizens to beautify the city and minister to their needs and pleasures by generous private contributions.

All these gifts were for the city of Rome, and for the people of the city, not for the Empire, nor for Italy. This is characteristic of ancient generosity or philanthropy, that its recipients are commonly the people of a single town, usually the donor's native town. It is one of many indications of the fact that the Roman thought of his city as the state, and even under the Empire he rarely extended the scope of his benefactions beyond the walls of a particular town. The small cities and villages throughout the West reproduced the capital in miniature. Each was a little world in itself. Each of them not only had its forum, its temples, colonnades, baths, theatres, and arenas, but also developed a political and social organization like that of the city of Rome. It had its own local chief magistrates, distinguished by their official robes and insignia of office, and its senators, who enjoyed the privilege of occupying special seats in the theatre, and it was natural that the common people at Ostia, Ariminum, or Lugudunum, like those at Rome, should expect from those whom fortune had favored some return for the distinctions which they enjoyed. In this way the prosperous in each little town came to feel a sense of obligation to their native place, and this feeling of civic pride and responsibility was strengthened by the same spirit of rivalry between different villages that the Italian towns of the Middle Ages seem to have inherited from their ancestors, a spirit of rivalry which made each one eager to surpass the others in its beauty and attractiveness. Perhaps there have never been so many beautiful towns in any other period in history as there were in the Roman Empire, during the second century of our era, and their attractive features--their colonnades, temples, fountains, and works of art--were due in large measure to the generosity of private citizens. We can make this statement with considerable confidence, because these benefactions are recorded for us on innumerable tablets of stone and bronze, scattered throughout the Empire.

These contributions not only helped to meet the cost of building temples, colonnades, and other structures, but they were often intended to cover a part of the running expenses of the city. This is one of the novel features of Roman municipal life. We can understand the motives which would lead a citizen of New York or Boston to build a museum or an arch in his native city. Such a structure would serve as a monument to him; it would give distinction to the city, and it would give him and his fellow citizens æsthetic satisfaction tion But if a rich New Yorker should give a large sum to mend the pavement in Union Square or extend the sewer system on Canal Street, a judicial inquiry into his sanity would not be thought out of place. But the inscriptions show us that rich citizens throughout the Roman Empire frequently made large contributions for just such unromantic purposes. It is unfortunate that a record of the annual income and expenses of some Italian or Gallic town has not come down to us. It would be interesting, for instance, to compare the budget of Mantua or Ancona, in the first century of our era, with that of Princeton or Cambridge in the twentieth. But, although we rarely know the sums which were expended for particular purposes, a mere comparison of the objects for which they were spent is illuminating. The items in the ancient budget which find no place in our own, and vice versa, are significant of certain striking differences between ancient and modern municipal life.

Common to the ancient and the modern city are expenditures for the construction and maintenance of public buildings, sewers, aqueducts, and streets, but with these items the parallelism ends. The ancient objects of expenditure which find no place in the budget of an American town are the repair of the town walls, the maintenance of public worship, the support of the baths, the sale of grain at a low price, and the giving of games and theatrical performances. It is very clear that the ancient legislator made certain provisions for the physical and spiritual welfare of his fellow citizens which find little or no place in our municipal arrangements to-day. If, among the sums spent for the various objects mentioned above, we compare the amounts set apart for religion and for the baths, we may come to the conclusion that the Roman read the old saying, "Cleanliness is next to godliness" in the amended form "Cleanliness is next above godliness." No city in the Empire seems to have been too small or too poor to possess public baths, and how large an item of annual expense their care was is clear from the fact that an article of the Theodosian code provided that cities should spend at least one-third of their incomes on the heating of the baths and the repair of the walls. The great idle population of the city of Rome had to be provided with food at public expense. Otherwise riot and disorder would have followed, but in the towns the situation was not so threatening, and probably furnishing grain to the people did not constitute a regular item of expense. So far as public entertainments were concerned, the remains of theatres and amphitheatres in Pompeii, Fiesole, Aries, Orange, and at many other places to-day furnish us visible evidence of the large sums which ancient towns must have spent on plays and gladiatorial games. In the city of Rome in the fourth century, there were one hundred and seventy-five days on which performances were given in the theatres, arenas, and amphitheatres.

We have been looking at the items which were peculiar to the ancient budget. Those which are missing from it are still more indicative, if possible, of differences between Roman character and modes of life and those of to-day. Provision was rarely made for schools, museums, libraries, hospitals, almshouses, or for the lighting of streets. No salaries were paid to city officials; no expenditure was made for police or for protection against fire, and the slaves whom every town owned probably took care of the public buildings and kept the streets clean. The failure of the ancient city government to provide for educational and charitable institutions, means, as we shall see later, that in some cases these matters were neglected, that in others they were left to private enterprise. It appears strange that the admirable police and fire system which Augustus introduced into Rome was not adopted throughout the Empire, but that does not seem to have been the case, and life and property must have been exposed to great risks, especially on festival days and in the unlighted streets at night. The rich man could be protected by his bodyguard of clients, and have his way lighted at night by the torches which his slaves carried, but the little shopkeeper must have avoided the dark alleys or attached himself to the retinue of some powerful man. Some of us will recall in this connection the famous wall painting at Pompeii which depicts the riotous contest between the Pompeians and the people of the neighboring town of Nuceria, at the Pompeian gladiatorial games in 50 B.C., when stones were thrown and weapons freely used. What scenes of violence and disorder there must have been on such occasions as these, without systematic police surveillance, can be readily imagined.

The sums of money which an ancient or a modern city spends fall in two categories--the amounts which are paid out for permanent improvements, and the running expenses of the municipality. We have just been looking at the second class of expenditures, and our brief examination of it shows clearly enough that the ancient city took upon its shoulders only a small part of the burden which a modern municipality assumes. It will be interesting now to see how far the municipal outlay for running expenses was supplemented by private generosity, and to find out the extent to which the cities were indebted to the same source for their permanent improvements. A great deal of light is thrown on these two questions by the hundreds of stone and bronze tablets which were set up by donors themselves or by grateful cities to commemorate the gifts made to them. The responsibility which the rich Roman felt to spend his money for the public good was unequivocally stated by the poet Martial in one of his epigrams toward the close of the first century of our era. The speaker in the poem tells his friend Pastor why he is striving to be rich--not that he may have broad estates, rich appointments, fine wines, or troops of slaves, but "that he may give and build for the public good" ("ut donem, Pastor, et ædificem"), and this feeling of stewardship found expression in a steady outpouring of gifts in the interests of the people.

The practice of giving may well have started with the town officials. We have already noticed that in Rome, under the Republic, candidates for office, in seeking votes, and magistrates, in return for the honors paid them, not infrequently spent large sums on the people. In course of time, in the towns throughout the Empire this voluntary practice became a legal obligation resting on local officials. This fact is brought out in the municipal charter of Urso,[95] the modern Osuna, in Spain. Half of this document, engraved on tablets, was discovered in Spain about forty years ago, and makes a very interesting contribution to our knowledge of municipal life. A colony was sent out to Urso, in 44 B.C., by Julius Cæsar, under the care of Mark Antony, and the municipal constitution of the colony was drawn up by one of these two men. In the seventieth article, we read of the duumvirs, who were the chief magistrates: "Whoever shall be duumvirs, with the exception of those who shall have first been elected after the passage of this law, let the aforesaid during their magistracy give a public entertainment or plays in honor of the gods and goddesses Jupiter, Juno, and Minerva, for four days, during the greater part of the day, so far as it may be done, at the discretion of the common councillors, and on these games and this entertainment let each one of them spend from his own money not less than two thousand sesterces." The article which follows in the document provides that the ædiles, or the officials next in rank, shall give gladiatorial games and plays for three days, and one day of races in the circus, and for these entertainments they also must spend not less than two thousand sesterces.

Here we see the modern practice reversed. City officials, instead of receiving a salary for their services, not only serve without pay, but are actually required by law to make a public contribution. It will be noticed that the law specified the minimum sum which a magistrate *must* spend. The people put no limit on what he *might* spend, and probably most of the duumvirs of Urso gave more than $80, or, making allowance for the difference in the purchasing value of money, $250, for the entertainment of the people. In fact a great many honorary inscriptions from other towns tell us of officials who made generous additions to the sum required by law. So far as their purpose and results go, these expenditures may be compared with the "campaign contributions" made by candidates for office in this country. There is a strange likeness and unlikeness between the two. The modern politician makes his contribution before the election, the ancient politician after it. In our day the money is expended largely to provide for public meetings where the questions of the day shall be discussed. In Roman times it was spent upon public improvements, and upon plays, dinners, and gladiatorial games. Among us public sentiment is averse to the expenditure of large sums to secure an election. The Romans desired and expected it, and those who were open-handed in this matter took care to have a record of their gifts set down where it could be read by all men.

On general grounds we should expect our system to have a better effect on the intelligence and character of the people, and to secure better officials. The discussion of public questions, even in a partisan way, brings them to the attention of the people, sets the people thinking, and helps to educate voters on political and economic matters. If we may draw an inference from the election posters in Pompeii, such subjects played a small part in a city election under the Empire. It must have been demoralizing, too, to a Pompeian or a citizen of Salona to vote for a candidate, not because he would make the most honest and able duumvir or ædile among the men canvassing for the office, but because he had the longest purse. How our sense of propriety would be shocked if the newly elected mayor of Hartford or Montclair should give a gala performance in the local theatre to his fellow-citizens or pay for a free exhibition by a circus troupe! But perhaps we should overcome our scruples and go, as the people of Pompeii did, and perhaps our consciences would be completely salved if the aforesaid mayor proceeded to lay a new pavement in Main Street, to erect a fountain on the Green, or stucco the city hall. Naturally only rich men could be elected to office in Roman towns, and in this respect the same advantages and disadvantages attach to the Roman system as we find in the practice which the English have followed up to the present time of paying no salary to members of the House of Commons, and in our own practice of letting our ambassadors meet a large part of their legitimate expenses.

The large gifts made to their native towns by rich men elected to public office set an example which private citizens of means followed in an extraordinary way. Sometimes they gave statues, or baths, or fountains, or porticos, and sometimes they provided for games, or plays, or dinners, or lottery tickets. Perhaps nothing can convey to our minds so clear an impression of the motives of the donors, the variety and number of the gifts, and their probable effect on the character of the people as to read two or three specimens of these dedicatory inscriptions. The citizens of Lanuvium, near Rome, set up a monument in honor of a certain Valerius, "because he cleaned out and restored the water courses for a distance of three miles, put the pipes in position again, and restored the two baths for men and the bath for women, all at his own expense."[96] A citizen of Sinuessa leaves this record: "Lucius Papius Pollio, the duumvir, to his father, Lucius Papius. Cakes and mead to all the citizens of Sinuessa and Cædici; gladiatorial games and a dinner for the people of Sinuessa and the Papian clan; a monument at a cost of 12,000 sesterces."[97] Such a catholic provision to suit all tastes should certainly have served to keep his father from being forgotten. A citizen of Beneventum lays claim to distinction because "he first scattered tickets among the people by means of which he distributed gold, silver, bronze, linen garments, and other things."[98] The people of Telesia, a little town in Campania, pay this tribute to their distinguished patron: "To Titus Fabius Severus, patron of the town, for his services at home and abroad, and because he, first of all those who have instituted games, gave at his own expense five wild beasts from Africa, a company of gladiators, and a splendid equipment, the senate and citizens have most gladly granted a statue."[99] The office of patron was a characteristic Roman institution. Cities and villages elected to this position some distinguished Roman senator or knight, and he looked out for the interests of the community in legal matters and otherwise.

This distinction was held in high esteem, and recipients of it often testified their appreciation by generous gifts to the town which they represented, or were chosen patrons because of their benefactions. This fact is illustrated in the following inscription from Spoletium: "Gaius Torasius Severus, the son of Gaius, of the Horatian tribe, quattuorvir with judicial power, augur, in his own name, and in the name of his son Publius Meclonius Proculus Torasianus, the pontiff, erected (this) on his land (?) and at his own expense. He also gave the people 250,000 sesterces to celebrate his son's birthday, from the income of which each year, on the third day before the Kalends of

September, the members of the Common Council are to dine in public, and each citizen who is present is to receive eight *asses*. He also gave to the seviri Augustales, and to the priests of the Lares, and to the overseers of the city wards, 120,000 sesterces, in order that from the income of this sum they might have a public dinner on the same day. Him, for his services to the community, the senate has chosen patron of the town."[100] A town commonly showed its appreciation of what had been done for it by setting up a statue in honor of its benefactor, as was done in the case of Fabius Severus, and the public squares of Italian and provincial towns must have been adorned with many works of art of this sort. It amuses one to find at the bottom of some of the commemorative tablets attached to these statues, the statement that the man distinguished in this way, "contented with the honor, has himself defrayed the cost of the monument." To pay for a popular testimonial to one's generosity is indeed generosity in its perfect form. The statues themselves have disappeared along with the towns which erected them, but the tablets remain, and by a strange dispensation of fate the monument which a town has set up to perpetuate the memory of one of its citizens is sometimes the only record we have of the town's own existence.

The motives which actuated the giver were of a mixed character, as these memorials indicate. Sometimes it was desire for the applause of his fellow citizens, or for posthumous fame, which influenced a donor; sometimes civic pride and affection. In many cases it was the compelling force of custom, backed up now and then, as we can see from the inscriptions, by the urgent demands of the populace. Out of this last sentiment there would naturally grow a sense of the obligation imposed by the possession of wealth, and this feeling is closely allied to pure generosity. In fact, it would probably be wrong not to count this among the original motives which actuated men in making their gifts, because the spirit of devotion to the state and to the community was a marked characteristic of Romans in the republican period.

The effects which this practice of giving had on municipal life and on the character of the people are not without importance and interest. The lavish expenditure expected of a magistrate and the ever-increasing financial obligations laid upon him by the central government made municipal offices such an intolerable burden that the charter of Urso of the first century A.D., which has been mentioned above, has to resort to various ingenious devices to compel men to hold them. The position of a member of a town council was still worse. He was not only expected to contribute generously to the embellishment and support of his native city, but he was also held responsible for the collection of the imperial taxes. As prosperity declined he found this an increasingly difficult thing to do, and seats in the local senate were undesirable. The central government could not allow the men responsible for its revenues to escape their responsibility. Consequently, it interposed and forced them to accept the honor. Some of them enlisted in the army, or even fled into the desert, but whenever they were found they were brought back to take up their positions again. In the fourth century, service in the common council was even made a penalty imposed upon criminals. Finally, it became hereditary, and it is an amusing but pathetic thing to find that this honor, so highly prized in the early period, became in the end a form of serfdom.

We have been looking at the effects of private generosity on official life. Its results for the private citizen are not so clear, but it must have contributed to that decline of independence and of personal responsibility which is so marked a feature of the later Empire. The masses contributed little, if anything, to the running expenses of government and the improvement of the city. The burdens fell largely upon the rich. It was a system of quasi-socialism. Those who had, provided for those who had not--not merely markets and temples, and colonnades, and baths, but oil for the baths, games, plays, and gratuities of money. Since their needs were largely met by others, the people lost more and more the habit of providing for themselves and the ability to do so. When prosperity declined, and the wealthy could no more assist them, the end came.

The objects for which donors gave their money seem to prove the essentially materialistic character of Roman civilization, because we must assume that those who gave knew the tastes of the people. Sometimes men like Pliny the Younger gave money for libraries or schools, but such gifts seem to have been relatively infrequent. Benefactions are commonly intended to satisfy the material needs or gratify the desire of the people for pleasure.

Under the old régime charity was unknown. There were neither almshouses nor hospitals, and scholars have called attention to the fact that even the doles of corn which the state gave were granted to citizens only. Mere residents or strangers were left altogether out of consideration, and they were rarely included within the scope of private benevolence. In the following chapter, in discussing the trades-guilds, we shall see that even they made no provision for the widow or orphan, or for their sick or disabled members. It was not until Christianity came that the poor and the needy were helped because of their poverty and need.

## Some Reflections on Corporations and Trades-Guilds

In a recent paper on "Ancient and Modern Imperialism," read before the British Classical Association, Lord Cromer, England's late consul-general in Egypt, notes certain points of resemblance between the English and the Roman methods of dealing with alien peoples. With the Greeks no such points of contact exist, because, as he remarks, "not only was the imperial idea foreign to the Greek mind; the federal conception was equally strange." This similarity between the political character and methods of the Romans and Anglo-Saxons strikes any one who reads the history of the two peoples side by side. They show the same genius for government at home, and a like success in conquering and holding foreign lands, and in assimilating alien peoples. Certain qualities which they have in common contribute to these like results. Both the Roman and the Anglo-Saxon have been men of affairs; both have shown great skill in adapting means to an end, and each has driven straight at the immediate object to be accomplished without paying much heed to logic or political theory. A Roman statesman would have said "Amen!" to the Englishman's pious hope that "his countrymen might never become consistent or logical in politics." Perhaps the willingness of the average Roman to co-operate with his fellows, and his skill in forming an organization suitable for the purpose in hand, go farther than any of the other qualities mentioned above to account for his success in governing other peoples as well as his own nation.

Our recognition of these striking points of resemblance between the Romans and ourselves has come from a comparative study of the political life of the two peoples. But the likeness to each other of the Romans and Anglo-Saxons, especially in the matter of associating themselves together for a common object, is still more apparent in their methods of dealing with private affairs. A characteristic and amusing illustration of the working of this tendency among the Romans is furnished by the early history of monasticism in the Roman world. When the Oriental Christian had convinced himself of the vanity of the world, he said: "It is the weakness of the flesh and the enticements of the wicked which tempt me to sin. Therefore I will withdraw from the world and mortify the flesh." This is the spirit which drove him into the desert or the mountains, to live in a cave with a lion or a wolf for his sole companion. This is the spirit which took St. Anthony into a solitary place in Egypt. It led St. Simeon Stylites to secure a more perfect sense of aloofness from the world, and a greater security from contact with it by spending the last thirty years of his life on the top of a pillar near Antioch. In the Western world, which was thoroughly imbued with the Roman spirit, the Christian who held the same view as his Eastern brother of the evil results flowing from intercourse with his fellow men, also withdrew from the world, but he withdrew in the company of a group of men who shared his opinions on the efficacy of a life of solitude. A delightful instance of the triumph of the principle of association over logic or theory! We Americans can understand perfectly the compelling force of the principle, even in such a case as this, and we should justify the Roman's action on the score of practical common sense. We have organizations for almost every conceivable political, social, literary, and economic purpose. In fact, it would be hard to mention an object for which it would not be possible to organize a club, a society, a league, a guild, or a union. In a similar way the Romans had organizations of capitalists and laborers, religious associations, political and social clubs, and leagues of veterans.

So far as organizations of capitalists are concerned, their history is closely bound up with that of imperialism. They come to our notice for the first time during the wars with Carthage, when Rome made her earliest acquisitions outside of Italy. In his account of the campaigns in Spain against Hannibal's lieutenants, Livy tells us[101] of the great straits to which the Roman army was reduced for its pay, food, and clothing. The need was urgent, but the treasury was empty, and the people poverty-stricken. In this emergency the prætor called a public meeting, laid before it the situation in Spain, and, appealing to the joint-stock companies to come to the relief of the state, appointed a day when proposals could be made to furnish what was required by the army. On the appointed day three *societates*, or corporations, offered to make the necessary loans to the government; their offers were accepted, and the needs of the army were met. The transaction reminds us of similar emergencies in our civil war, when syndicates of bankers came to the support of the government. The present-day tendency to question the motives of all corporations dealing with the government does not seem to color Livy's interpretation of the incident, for he cites it in proof of the patriotic spirit which ran through all classes in the face of the struggle with Carthage. The appearance of the joint-stock company at the moment when the policy of territorial expansion is coming to the front is significant of the close connection which existed later between imperialism and corporate finance, but the later relations of corporations to the public interests cannot always be interpreted in so charitable a fashion.

Our public-service companies find no counter-part in antiquity, but the Roman societies for the collection of taxes bear a resemblance to these modern organizations of capital in the nature of the franchises, as we may call them, and the special privileges which they had. The practice which the Roman government followed of letting out to the highest bidder the privilege of collecting the taxes in each of the provinces, naturally gave a great impetus to the development of companies organized for this purpose. Every new province added to the Empire opened a fresh field for capitalistic enterprise, in the way not only of farming the taxes, but also of loaning money, constructing public works, and leasing the mines belonging to the state, and Roman politicians must have felt these financial considerations steadily pushing them on to further conquests.

But the interest of the companies did not end when Roman eagles had been planted in a new region. It was necessary to have the provincial government so managed as to help the agents of the companies in making as much money as possible out of the provincials, and Cicero's year as governor of Cilicia was made almost intolerable by the exactions which these agents practised on the Cilicians, and the pressure which they brought to bear upon him and his subordinates. His letters to his intimate friend, Atticus, during this period contain pathetic accounts of the embarrassing situations in which loaning companies and individual capitalists at Rome placed him. On one occasion a certain Scaptius came to him[102], armed with a strong letter of recommendation from the impeccable Brutus, and asked to be appointed prefect of Cyprus. His purpose was, by official pressure, to squeeze out of the people of Salamis, in Cyprus, a debt which they owed, running at forty-eight per cent interest. Upon making some inquiry into the previous history of Scaptius, Cicero learned that under his predecessor in Cilicia, this same Scaptius had secured an appointment as prefect of Cyprus, and backed by his official power, to collect money due his company, had shut up the members of the Salaminian common council in their town hall until five of them died of starvation. In domestic politics the companies played an equally important rôle. The relations which existed between the "interests" and political leaders were as close in ancient times as they are to-day, and corporations were as unpartisan in Rome in their political alliances as they are in the United States. They impartially supported the democratic platforms of Gaius Gracchus and Julius Cæsar in return for valuable concessions, and backed the candidacy of the constitutionalist Pompey for the position of commander-in-chief of the fleets and armies acting against the Eastern pirates, and against Mithridates, in like expectation of substantial returns for their help. What gave the companies their influence at the polls was the fact that their shares were very widely held by voters. Polybius, the Greek historian, writing of conditions at Rome in the second century B.C., gives us to understand that almost every citizen owned shares in some joint-stock company[103]. Poor crops in Sicily, heavy rains in Sardinia, an uprising in Gaul, or "a strike" in the Spanish mines would touch the pocket of every middle-class Roman.

In these circumstances it is hard to see how the Roman got on without stock quotations in the newspapers. But Cæsar's publication of the *Acta Diurna*, or proceedings of the senate and assembly, would take the place of our newspapers in some respects, and the crowds which gathered at the points where these documents were posted, would remind us of the throngs collected in front of the bulletin in the window of a newspaper office when some exciting event has occurred. Couriers were constantly arriving from the agents of corporations in Gaul, Spain, Africa, and Asia with the latest news of industrial and financial enterprises in all these sections. What a scurrying of feet there must have been through the streets when the first news reached Rome of the insurrection of the proletariat in Asia in 88 B.C., and of the proclamation of Mithridates guaranteeing release from half of their obligations to all debtors who should kill money-lenders! Asiatic stocks must have dropped almost to the zero point. We find no evidence of the existence of an organized stock exchange. Perhaps none was necessary, because the shares of stock do not seem to have been transferable, but other financial business arising out of the organization of these companies, like the loaning of money on stock, could be transacted reasonably well in the row of banking offices which ran along one side of the Forum, and made it an ancient Wall Street or Lombard Street.

"Trusts" founded to control prices troubled the Romans, as they trouble us to-day. There is an amusing reference to one of these trade combinations as early as the third century before our era in the Captives of Plautus.[104] The parasite in the play has been using his best quips and his most effective leads to get an invitation to dinner, but he can't provoke a smile, to say nothing of extracting an invitation. In a high state of indignation he threatens to prosecute the men who avoid being his hosts for entering into an unlawful combination like that of "the oil dealers in the Velabrum." Incidentally it is a rather interesting historical coincidence that the pioneer monopoly in Rome, as in our day, was an oil trust--in the time of Plautus, of course, an olive-oil trust. In the "Trickster," which was presented in 191 B.C., a character refers to the mountains of grain which the dealers had in their warehouses.[105] Two years later the "corner" had become so effective that the government intervened, and the curule ædiles who had charge of the markets imposed a heavy fine on the grain speculators.[106] The case was apparently prosecuted under the Laws of the Twelve Tables of 450 B.C., the Magna Charta of Roman liberty. It would seem, therefore, that combinations in restraint of trade were formed at a very early date in Rome, and perhaps Diocletian's attempt in the third century of our era to lower the cost of living by fixing the prices of all sorts of commodities was aimed in part at the same evil. As for government ownership, the Roman state made one or two essays in this field, notably in the case of mines, but with indifferent success.

Labor was as completely organized as capital.[107] In fact the passion of the Romans for association shows itself even more clearly here, and it would be possible to write their industrial history from a study of their trades-unions. The story of Rome carries the founding of these guilds back to the early days of the regal period. From the investigations of Waltzing, Liebenam, and others their history can be made out in considerable detail. Roman tradition was delightfully systematic in assigning the founding of one set of institutions to one king and of another group to another king. Romulus, for instance, is the war king, and concerns himself with military and political institutions. The second king, Numa, is a man of peace, and is occupied throughout his reign with the social and religious organization of his people. It was Numa who established guilds of carpenters, dyers, shoemakers, tanners, workers in copper and gold, fluteplayers, and potters. The critical historian looks with a sceptical eye on the story of the kings, and yet this list of trades is just what we should expect to find in primitive Rome. There are no bakers or weavers, for instance, in the list. We know that in our own colonial days the baking, spinning, and weaving were done at home, as they would naturally have been when Rome was a community of shepherds and farmers. As Roman civilization became more complex, industrial specialization developed, and the number of guilds grew, but during the Republic we cannot trace their growth very successfully for lack of information about them. Corporations, as we have seen, played an important part in politics, and their doings are chronicled in the literature, like oratory and history, which deals with public questions, but the trades-guilds had little share in politics; they were made up of the obscure and weak, and consequently are rarely mentioned in the writings of a Cicero or a Livy.

It is only when the general passion for setting down records of all sorts of enterprises and incidents on imperishable materials came in with the Empire that the story of the Roman trades-union can be clearly followed. It is a fortunate thing for us that this mania swept through the Roman Empire, because it has given us some twenty-five hundred inscriptions dealing with these organizations of workmen. These inscriptions disclose the fact that there were more than eighty different trades organized into guilds in the city of Rome alone. They included skilled and unskilled laborers, from the porters, or *saccarii*, to the goldsmiths, or *aurifices*. The names of some of them, like the *pastillarii*, or guild of pastile-makers, and the *scabillarii*, or castanet-players, indicate a high degree of industrial specialization. From one man's tombstone even the conclusion seems to follow that he belonged to a union of what we may perhaps call checker-board makers. The merchants formed trade associations freely. Dealers in oil, in wine, in fish, and in grain are found organized all over the Empire. Even the perfumers, hay-dealers, and ragmen had their societies. No line of distinction seems to be drawn between the artist and the artisan. The mason and the sculptor were classed in the same category by Roman writers, so that we are not surprised to find unions of men in both occupations. A curious distinction between the professions is also brought out by these guild inscriptions. There are unions made up of physicians, but none of lawyers, for the lawyer in early times was supposed to receive no remuneration for his services. In point of fact the physician was on a lower social plane in Rome than he was even among our ancestors. The profession was followed almost exclusively by Greek freedmen, as we can see from the records on their tombstones, and was highly specialized, if we may judge from the epitaphs of eye and ear doctors, surgeons, dentists, and veterinarians. To the same category with the physician and sculptor belong the architect, the teacher, and the chemist. Men of these professions pursued the *artes liberales*, as the Romans put it, and constituted an aristocracy among those engaged in the trades or lower professions. Below them in the hierarchy came those who gained a livelihood by the *artes ludicræ*, like the actor, professional dancer, juggler, or gladiator, and in the lowest caste were the carpenters, weavers, and other artisans whose occupations were *artes vulgares et sordidæ*.

In the early part of this chapter the tendency of the Romans to form voluntary associations was noted as a national characteristic. This fact comes out very clearly if we compare the number of trades-unions in the Western world with those in Greece and the Orient. Our conclusions must be drawn of course from the extant inscriptions which refer to guilds, and time may have dealt more harshly with the stones in one place than in another, or the Roman government may have given its consent to the establishment of such organizations with more reluctance in one province than another; but, taking into account the fact that we have guild inscriptions from four hundred and seventy-five towns and villages in the Empire, these elements of uncertainty in our conclusions are practically eliminated, and a fair comparison may be drawn between conditions in the East and the West. If we pick out some of the more important towns in the Greek part of the Roman world, we find five guilds reported from Tralles in Caria, six from Smyrna, one from Alexandria, and eleven from Hierapolis in Phrygia. On the other hand, in the city of Rome there were more than one hundred, in Brixia (modern Brescia) seventeen or more, in Lugudunum (Lyons) twenty at least, and in Canabæ, in the province of Dacia, five. These figures, taken at random for some of the larger towns in different parts of the Empire, bring out the fact very clearly that the western and northern provinces readily accepted Roman ideas and showed the Roman spirit, as illustrated in their ability and willingness to co-operate for a common purpose, but that the Greek East was never Romanized. Even in the settlements in Dacia, which continued under Roman rule only from 107 to 270 A.D., we find as many trades-unions as existed in Greek towns which were held by the Romans for three or four centuries. The comparative number of guilds and of guild inscriptions would, in fact, furnish us with a rough test of the extent to which Rome impressed her civilization on different parts of the Empire, even if we had no other criteria. We should know, for instance, that less progress had been made in Britain than in Southern Gaul, that Salona in Dalmatia, Lugudunum in Gaul, and Mogontiacum (Mainz) in Germany were important centres of Roman civilization. It is, of course, possible from a study of these inscriptions to make out the most flourishing industries in the several towns, but with that we are not concerned here.

These guilds which we have been considering were trades-unions in the sense that they were organizations made up of men working in the same trade, but they differed from modern unions, and also from mediaeval guilds, in the objects for which they were formed. They made no attempt to raise wages, to improve working conditions, to limit the number of apprentices, to develop skill and artistic taste in the craft, or to better the social or political position of the laborer. It was the need which their members felt for companionship, sympathy, and help in the emergencies of life, and the desire to give more meaning to their lives, that drew them together. These motives explain the provisions made for social gatherings, and for the burial of members, which were the characteristic features of most of the organizations. It is the social side, for instance, which is indicated on a tombstone, found in a little town of central Italy. After giving the name of the deceased, it reads: "He bequeathed to his guild, the rag-dealers, a thousand sesterces, from the income of which each year, on the festival of the Parentalia, not less than twelve men shall dine at his tomb."[108] Another in northern Italy reads: "To Publius Etereius Quadratus, the son of Publius, of the *Tribus Quirina,* Etereia Aristolais, his mother, has set up a statue, at whose dedication she gave the customary banquet to the union of rag-dealers, and also a sum of money, from the income of which annually, from this time forth, on the birthday of Quadratus, April 9, where his remains have been laid, they should make a sacrifice, and should hold the customary banquet in the temple, and should bring roses in their season and cover and crown the statue; which thing they have undertaken to do."[109] The menu of one of these dinners given in Dacia[110] has come down to us. It includes lamb and pork, bread, salad, onions, and two kinds of wine. The cost of the entertainment amounted to one hundred and sixty-nine *denarii,* or about twenty-seven dollars, a sum which would probably have a purchasing value to-day of from three to four times that amount.

The "temple" or chapel referred to in these inscriptions was usually semicircular, and may have served as a model for the Christian oratories. The building usually stood in a little grove, and, with its accommodations for official meetings and dinners, served the same purpose as a modern club-house. Besides the special gatherings for which some deceased member or some rich patron provided, the guild met at fixed times during the year to dine or for other social purposes. The income of the society, which was made up of the initiation fees and monthly dues of the members, and of donations, was supplemented now and then by a system of fines. At least, in an

African inscription we read: "In the Curia of Jove. Done November 27, in the consulship of Maternus and Atticus.... If any one shall wish to be a flamen, he shall give three amphorae of wine, besides bread and salt and provisions. If any one shall wish to be a magister, he shall give two amphorae of wine.... If any one shall have spoken disrespectfully to a flamen, or laid hands upon him, he shall pay two denarii.... If any one shall have gone to fetch wine, and shall have made away with it, he shall give double the amount."[111]

The provision which burial societies made for their members is illustrated by the following epitaph:

"To the shade of Gaius Julius Filetio, born in Africa, a physician, who lived thirty-five years. Gaius Julius Filetus and Julia Euthenia, his parents, have erected it to their very dear son. Also to Julius Athenodorus, his brother, who lived thirty-five years. Euthenia set it up. He has been placed here, to whose burial the guild of rag-dealers has contributed three hundred denarii."[112] People of all ages have craved a respectable burial, and the pathetic picture which Horace gives us in one of his Satires of the fate which befell the poor and friendless at the end of life, may well have led men of that class to make provisions which would protect them from such an experience, and it was not an unnatural thing for these organizations to be made up of men working in the same trade. The statutes of several guilds have come down to us. One found at Lanuvium has articles dealing particularly with burial regulations. They read in part:[113]

"It has pleased the members, that whoever shall wish to join this guild shall pay an initiation fee of one hundred sesterces, and an amphora of good wine, as well as five *asses* a month. Voted likewise, that if any man shall not have paid his dues for six consecutive months, and if the lot common to all men has befallen him, his claim to a burial shall not be considered, even if he shall have so stipulated in his will. Voted likewise, that if any man from this body of ours, having paid his dues, shall depart, there shall come to him from the treasury three hundred sesterces, from which sum fifty sesterces, which shall be divided at the funeral pyre, shall go for the funeral rites. Furthermore, the obsequies shall be performed on foot."

Besides the need of comradeship, and the desire to provide for a respectable burial, we can see another motive which brought the weak and lowly together in these associations. They were oppressed by the sense of their own insignificance in society, and by the pitifully small part which they played in the affairs of the world. But if they could establish a society of their own, with concerns peculiar to itself which they would administer, and if they could create positions of honor and importance in this organization, even the lowliest man in Rome would have a chance to satisfy that craving to exercise power over others which all of us feel, to hold titles and distinctions, and to wear the insignia of office and rank. This motive worked itself out in the establishment of a complete hierarchy of offices, as we saw in part in an African inscription given above. The Roman state was reproduced in miniature in these societies, with their popular assemblies, and their officials, who bore the honorable titles of quæstor, curator, prætor, ædile, and so forth.

To read these twenty-five hundred or more inscriptions from all parts of the Empire brings us close to the heart of the common people. We see their little ambitions, their jealousies, their fears, their gratitude for kindness, their own kindliness, and their loyalty to their fellows. All of them are anxious to be remembered after death, and provide, when they can do so, for the celebration of their birthdays by members of the association. A guild inscription in Latium, for instance, reads:[114] "Jan. 6, birthday of Publius Claudius Veratius Abascantianus, [who has contributed] 6,000 sesterces, [paying an annual interest of] 180 denarii." "Jan. 25, birthday of Gargilius Felix, [who has contributed] 2,000 sesterces, [paying an annual interest of] 60 denarii," and so on through the twelve months of the year.

It is not entirely clear why the guilds never tried to bring pressure to bear on their employers to raise wages, or to improve their position by means of the strike, or by other methods with which we are familiar to-day. Perhaps the difference between the ancient and modern methods of manufacture helps us to understand this fact. In modern times most articles can be made much more cheaply by machinery than by hand, and the use of water-power, of steam, and of electricity, and the invention of elaborate machines, has led us to bring together a great many workmen under one roof or in one factory. The men who are thus employed in a single establishment work under common conditions, suffer the same disadvantages, and are brought into such close relations with one another that common action to improve their lot is natural. In ancient times, as may be seen in the chapter on Diocletian's edict, machinery was almost unknown, and artisans worked singly in their own homes or in the houses of their employers, so that joint action to improve their condition would hardly be expected.

Another factor which should probably be taken into account is the influence of slavery. This institution did not play the important rôle under the Empire in depressing the free laborer which it is often supposed to have played, because it was steadily dying out; but an employer could always have recourse to slave labor to a limited extent, and the struggling freedmen who had just come up from slavery were not likely to urge very strongly their claims for consideration.

In this connection it is interesting to recall the fact that before slavery got a foothold in Rome, the masses in their struggle with the classes used what we think of to-day as the most modern weapon employed in industrial warfare. We can all remember the intense interest with which we watched the novel experience which St. Petersburg underwent some six years ago, when the general strike was instituted. And yet, if we accept tradition, that method of bringing the government and society to terms was used twice by the Roman proletariat over two thousand years ago. The plebeians, so the story goes, unable to get their economic and political rights, stopped work and withdrew from the city to the Sacred Mount. Their abstention from labor did not mean the going out of street lamps, the suspension of street-car traffic, and the closing of factories and shops, but, besides the loss of fighting men, it meant that no more shoes could be had, no more carpentry work done, and no more wine-jars made until concessions should be granted. But, having slaves to compete with it, and with conditions which made organization difficult, free labor could not hope to rise, and the unions could take no serious step toward the improvement of the condition of their members. The feeling of security on this score which society had, warranted the government in allowing even its own employees to organize, and we find unions of government clerks, messengers, and others. The Roman government was, therefore, never called upon to solve the grave political and economic questions which France and Italy have had to face in late years in the threatened strikes of the state railway and postal employees.

We have just been noticing how the ancient differed from the modern trades-union in the objects which it sought to obtain. The religious character which it took seems equally strange to us at first sight. Every guild put itself under the protection of some deity and was closely associated with a cult. Silvanus, the god of the woods, was a natural favorite with the carpenters, Father Bacchus with the innkeepers, Vesta with the bakers, and Diana with those who hunted wild animals for the circus. The reason for the choice of certain other divine patrons is not so clear. Why the cabmen of Tibur, for instance, picked out Hercules as their tutelary deity, unless, like Horace in his Satires, the ancient cabman thought of him as the god of treasure-trove, and, therefore, likely to inspire the giving of generous tips, we cannot guess. The religious side of Roman trade associations will not surprise us when we recall the strong religious bent of the Roman character, and when we remember that no body of Romans would have thought of forming any kind of an organization without securing the sanction and protection of the gods. The family, the clan, the state all had their protecting deities, to whom appropriate rites were paid on stated occasions. Speaking of the religious side of these trade organizations naturally reminds one of the religious associations which sprang up in such large numbers toward the end of the republican period and under the Empire. They lie outside the scope of this chapter, but, in the light of the issue which has arisen in recent years between religious associations and the governments of Italy, France, Spain, and Portugal, it is interesting to notice in passing that the Roman state strove to hold in check many of the ancient religious associations, but not always with much success. As we have noticed, its attitude toward the trade-guilds was not unfriendly. In the last days of the Republic, however, they began to enter politics, and were used very effectively in the elections by political leaders in both parties.[115] In fact the fortunes of the city seemed likely to be controlled by political clubs, until severe legislation and the transfer of the elections in the early Empire from the popular assemblies to the senate put an end to the use of trade associations for political purposes. It was in the light of this development that the government henceforth required all newly formed trades-unions to secure official authorization.

The change in the attitude of the state toward these organizations, as time went on, has been traced by Liebenam in his study of Roman associations. The story of this change furnishes an interesting episode in the history of special privilege, and may not be without profit to us. The Roman government started with the assumption that the operation of these voluntary associations was a matter of public as well as of private concern, and could serve public interests. Therefore their members were to be exempted from some of the burdens which the ordinary citizen bore. It was this reasoning, for instance, which led Trajan to set the bakers free from certain charges, and which influenced Hadrian to grant the same favors to those associations of skippers which supplied Rome with food. In the light of our present-day discussion it is interesting also to find that Marcus Aurelius granted them the right to manumit slaves and receive legacies--that is, he made them juridical persons. But if these associations were to be fostered by law, in proportion as they promoted the public welfare, it also followed logically that the state could put a restraining hand upon them when their development failed to serve public interests in the highest degree. Following this logical sequence, the Emperor Claudius, in his efforts to promote a more wholesome home life, or for some other reason not known to us, forbade the eating-houses or the delicatessen shops to sell cooked meats or warm water. Antoninus Pius, in his paternal care for the unions, prescribed an age test and a physical test for those who wished to become members. Later, under the law a man was allowed to join one guild only. Such a legal provision as this was a natural concomitant of the concession of privileges to the unions. If the members of these organizations were to receive special favors from the state, the state must see to it that the rolls were not padded. It must, in fact, have the right of final supervision of the list of members. So long as industry flourished, and so long as the population increased, or at least remained stationary, this oversight by the government brought no appreciable ill results. But when financial conditions grew steadily worse, when large tracts of land passed out of cultivation and the population rapidly dwindled, the numbers in the trades-unions began to decline. The public services, constantly growing heavier, which the state required of the guilds in return for their privileges made the loss of members still greater. This movement threatened the industrial interests of the Empire and must be checked at all hazards. Consequently, taking another logical step in the way of government regulation in the interests of the public, the state forbade men to withdraw from the unions, and made membership in a union hereditary. Henceforth the carpenter must always remain a carpenter, the weaver a weaver, and the sons and grandsons of the carpenter and the weaver must take up the occupation of their fathers, and a man is bound forever to his trade as the serf is to the soil.

## A Roman Politician

## (Gaius Scribonius Curio)

The life of Gaius Scribonius Curio has so many points of interest for the student of Roman politics and society, that one is bewildered by the variety of situations and experiences which it covers. His private character is made up of a *mélange* of contradictory qualities, of generosity, and profligacy, of sincerity and unscrupulousness. In his public life there is the same facile change of guiding principles. He is alternately a follower of Cicero and a supporter of his bitterest enemy, a Tory and a Democrat, a recognized opponent of Cæsar and his trusted agent and adviser. His dramatic career stirs Lucan to one of his finest passages, gives a touch of vigor to the prosaic narrative of Velleius, and even leads the sedate Pliny to drop into satire.[116] Friend and foe have helped to paint the picture. Cicero, the counsellor of his youth, writes of him and to him; Cælius, his bosom friend, analyzes his character; Cæsar leaves us a record of his military campaigns and death, while Velleius and Appian recount his public and private sins. His story has this peculiar charm, that many of the incidents which make it up are related from day to day, as they occurred, by his contemporaries, Cicero and Cælius, in the confidential letters which they wrote to their intimate friends. With all the strange elements which entered into it, however, his career is not an unusual one for the time in which he lived. Indeed it is almost typical for the class to which he belonged, and in studying it we shall come to know something more of that group of brilliant young men, made up of Cælius, Antony, Dolabella, and others, who were drawn to Cæsar's cause and played so large a part in bringing him success. The life of Curio not only illuminates social conditions in the first century before our era, but it epitomizes and personifies the political history of his time and the last struggles of the Republic. It brings within its compass the Catilinarian conspiracy, the agitation of Clodius, the formation of the first triumvirate, the rivalry of Cæsar and Pompey, and the civil war, for in all these episodes Curio took an active part.

Students of history have called attention to the striking way in which the members of certain distinguished Roman families from generation to generation kept up the political traditions of the family. The Claudian family is a striking case in point. Recognition of this fact helps us to understand Curio. His grandfather and his father were both prominent orators and politicians, as Cicero tells us in his

Brutus.[117] The grandfather reached the praetorship in the year in which Gaius Gracchus was done to death by his political opponents, while Curio pater was consul, in 76 B.C., when the confusion which followed the breaking up of the constitution and of the party of Sulla was at its height. Cicero tells us that the second Curio had "absolutely no knowledge of letters," but that he was one of the successful public speakers of his day, thanks to the training which he had received at home. The third Curio, with whom we are concerned here, was prepared for public life as his father had been, for Cicero remarks of him that "although he had not been sufficiently trained by teachers, he had a rare gift for oratory."[118]

On this point Cicero could speak with authority, because Curio had very possibly been one of his pupils in oratory and law. At least the very intimate acquaintance which he has with Curio's character and the incidents of his life, the fatherly tone of Cicero's letters to him, and the fact that Curio's nearest friends were among his disciples make this a natural inference. How intimate this relation was, one can see from the charming picture which Cicero draws, in the introductory chapters of his Essay on Friendship, of his own intercourse as a young man with the learned Augur Scævola. Roman youth attended their counsellor and friend when he went to the forum to take part in public business, or sat with him at home discussing matters of public and private interest, as Cicero and his companions sat on the bench in the garden with the pontiff Scævola, when he set forth the discourse of Lælius on friendship, and thus, out of his experience, the old man talked to the young men about him upon the conduct of life as well as upon the technical points of law and oratory. So many of the brilliant young politicians of this period had been brought into close relations with Cicero in this way, that when he found himself forced out of politics by the Cæsarians, he whimsically writes to his friend Pætus that he is inclined to give up public life and open a school, and not more than a year before his death he pathetically complains that he has not leisure even to take the waters at the spa, because of the demands which are made upon him for lessons in oratory.

If it did not take us too far from our chosen subject, it would be interesting to stop and consider at length what effect Cicero's intimate relations with these young men had upon his character, his political views, his personal fortunes, and the course of politics. That they kept him young in his interests and sympathies, that they kept his mind alert and receptive, comes out clearly in his letters to them, which are full of jest and raillery and enthusiasm. That he never developed into a Tory, as Catulus did, or became indifferent to political conditions, as Lucullus did, may have been due in part to his intimate association with this group of enthusiastic young politicians. So far as his personal fortunes were concerned, when the struggle between Cæsar and Pompey came, these former pupils of Cicero had an opportunity to show their attachment and their gratitude to him. *They* were followers of Cæsar, and *he* cast in his lot with Pompey. But this made no difference in their relations. To the contrary, they gave him advice and help; in their most hurried journeys they found time to visit him, and they interceded with Cæsar in his behalf. To determine whether he influenced the fortunes of the state through the effect which his teachings had upon these young men would require a paper by itself. Perhaps no man has ever had a better opportunity than Cicero had in their cases to leave a lasting impression on the political leaders of the coming generation. Curio, Cælius, Trebatius, Dolabella, Hirtius, and Pansa, who were Cæsar's lieutenants, in the years when their characters were forming and their political tendencies were being determined, were moulded by Cicero. They were warmly attached to him as their guide, philosopher, and friend, and they admired him as a writer, an orator, and an accomplished man of the world. Later they attached themselves to Cæsar, and while they were still under his spell, Cicero's influence over their political course does not seem to count for so much, but after Cæsar's death, the latent effect of Cicero's friendship and teaching makes itself clearly felt in the heroic service which such men as Hirtius and Pansa rendered to the cause of the dying Republic. Possibly even Curio, had he been living, might have been found, after the Ides of March, fighting by the side of Cicero.

Perhaps there is no better way of bringing out the intimate relations which Curio and the other young men of this group bore to the orator than by translating one of Cicero's early letters to him. It was written in 53 B.C., when the young man was in Asia, just beginning his political career as quæstor, or treasurer, on the staff of the governor of that province, and reads:[119]

"Although I grieve to have been suspected of neglect by you, still it has not been so annoying to me that my failure in duty is complained of by you as pleasant that it has been noticed, especially since, in so far as I am accused, I am free from fault. But in so far as you intimate that you long for a letter from me, you disclose that which I know well, it is true, but that which is sweet and cherished--

your love, I mean. In point of fact, I never let any one pass, who I think will go to you, without giving him a letter. For who is so indefatigable in writing as I am? From you, on the other hand, twice or thrice at most have I received a letter, and then a very short one. Therefore, if you are an unjust judge toward me, I shall condemn you on the same charge, but if you shall be unwilling to have me do that, you must show yourself just to me.

"But enough about letters; I have no fear of not satisfying you by writing, especially if in that kind of activity you will not scorn my efforts. I *did* grieve that you were away from us so long, inasmuch as I was deprived of the enjoyment of most delightful companionship, but now I rejoice because, in your absence, you have attained all your ends without sacrificing your dignity in the slightest degree, and because in all your undertakings the outcome has corresponded to my desires. What my boundless affection for you forces me to urge upon you is briefly put. So great a hope is based, shall I say, on your spirit or on your abilities, that I do not hesitate to beseech and implore you to come back to us with a character so moulded that you may be able to preserve and maintain this confidence in you which you have aroused. And since forgetfulness shall never blot out my remembrance of your services to me, I beg you to remember that whatever improvements may come in your fortune, or in your station in life, you would not have been able to secure them, if you had not as a boy in the old days followed my most loyal and loving counsels. Wherefore you ought to have such a feeling toward us, that we, who are now growing heavy with years, may find rest in your love and your youth."

In a most unexpected place, in one of Cicero's fiery invectives against Antony,[120] we come upon an episode illustrating his affectionate care of Curio during Curio's youth. The elder Curio lies upon a couch, prostrate with grief at the wreck which his son has brought on the house by his dissolute life and his extravagance. The younger Curio throws himself at Cicero's feet in tears. Like a foster-father, Cicero induces the young man to break off his evil habits, and persuades the father to forgive him and pay his debts. This scene which he describes here, reminds us of Curio's first appearance in Cicero's correspondence, where, with Curio's wild life in mind, he is spoken of as *filiola Curionis*.[121]

It is an appropriate thing that a man destined to lead so stormy a life as Curio did, should come on the stage as a leader in the wild turmoil of the Clodian affair. What brought the two Curios to the front in this matter as champions of Cicero's future enemy Clodius, it is not easy to say. It is interesting to notice in passing, however, that our Curio enters politics as a Democrat. He was the leader, in fact, of the younger element in that party, of the "Catilinarian crowd," as Cicero styles them, and arrayed himself against Lucullus, Hortensius, Messala, and other prominent Conservatives. What the methods were which Curio and his followers adopted, Cicero graphically describes.[122] They blocked up the entrances to the polling places with professional rowdies, and allowed only one kind of ballots to be distributed to the voters. This was in 61 B.C., when Curio can scarcely have been more than twenty-three years old.

In the following year Cæsar was back in Rome from his successful proprætorship in Spain, and found little difficulty in persuading Pompey and Crassus to join him in forming that political compact which controlled the fortunes of Rome for the next ten years. As a part of the agreement, Cæsar was made consul in 59 B.C., and forced his radical legislation through the popular assembly in spite of the violent opposition of the Conservatives. This is the year, too, of the candidacy of Clodius for the tribunate. Toward both these movements the attitude of Curio is puzzling. He reports to Cicero[123] that Clodius's main object in running for the tribunate is to repeal the legislation of Cæsar. It is strange that a man who had been in the counsels of Clodius, and was so shrewd on other occasions in interpreting political motives, can have been so deceived. We can hardly believe that he was double-faced toward Cicero. We must conclude, I think, that his strong dislike for Cæsar's policy and political methods colored his view of the situation. His fierce opposition to Cæsar is the other strange incident in this period of his life. Most of the young men of the time, even those of good family, were enthusiastic supporters of Cæsar. Curio, however, is bitterly opposed to him.[124] Perhaps he resented Cæsar's repression of freedom of speech, for he tells Cicero that the young men of Rome will not submit to the high-handed methods of the triumvirs, or perhaps he imbibed his early dislike for Cæsar from his father, whose sentiments are made clear enough by a savage epigram at Cæsar's expense, which Suetonius quotes from a speech of the elder Curio.[125] At all events he is the only man who dares speak out. He is the idol of the Conservatives, and is surrounded by enthusiastic crowds whenever he appears in the forum. He is now the recognized leader of the opposition to Cæsar, and a significant proof of this fact is furnished at the great games given in honor of Apollo in the summer of 59. When Cæsar entered the theatre there was faint applause; when Curio entered the crowd rose and cheered him, "as they used to cheer Pompey when the commonwealth was safe."[126] Perhaps the mysterious Vettius episode, an ancient Titus Oates affair, which belongs to this year, reflects the desire of the triumvirs to get rid of Curio, and shows also their fear of his opposition. This unscrupulous informer is said to have privately told Curio of a plot against the life of Pompey, in the hope of involving him in the meshes of the plot. Curio denounced him to Pompey, and Vettius was thrown into prison, where he was afterward found dead, before the truth of the matter could be brought out. Of course Curio's opposition to Cæsar effected little, except, perhaps, in drawing Cæsar's attention to him as a clever politician.

To Curio's quæstorship in Asia reference has already been made. It fell in 53 B.C., and from his incumbency of this office we can make an approximate estimate of his date of birth. Thirty or thirty-one was probably the minimum age for holding the quæstorship at this time, so that Curio must have been born about 84 B.C. From Cicero's letter to him, which has been given above, it would seem to follow that he had performed his duties in his province with eminent success. During his absence from Rome his father died, and with his father's death one stimulating cause of his dislike for Cæsar may have disappeared. To Curio's absence in his province we owe six of the charming letters which Cicero wrote to him. In one of his letters of this year he writes:[127] "There are many kinds of letters, as you well know, but one sort, for the sake of which letter-writing was invented, is best recognized: I mean letters written for the purpose of informing those who are not with us of whatever it may be to our advantage or to theirs that they should know. Surely you are not looking for a letter of this kind from me, for you have correspondents and messengers from home who report to you about your household. Moreover, so far as my concerns go, there is absolutely nothing new. There are two kinds of letters left which please me very much: one, of the informal and jesting sort; the other, serious and weighty. I do not feel that it is unbecoming to adopt either of these styles. Am I to jest with you by letter? On my word I do not think that there is a citizen who can laugh in these days. Or shall I write something of a more serious character? What subject is there on which Cicero can write seriously to Curio, unless it be concerning the commonwealth? And on this matter this is my situation: that I neither dare to set down in writing that which I think, nor wish to write what I do not think."

The Romans felt the same indifference toward affairs in the provinces that we show in this country, unless their investments were in danger. They were wrapped up in their own concerns, and politics in Rome were so absorbing in 53 B.C. that people in the city probably paid little attention to the doings of a quæstor in the far-away province of Asia. But, as the time for Curio's return approached, men recalled the striking rôle which he played in politics in earlier days, and wondered what course he would take when he came back. Events were moving rapidly toward a crisis. Julia, Cæsar's daughter, whom Pompey had married, died in the summer of 54 B.C., and Crassus was defeated and murdered by the Parthians in 53 B.C. The death of Crassus brought Cæsar and Pompey face to face, and Julia's death broke one of the strongest bonds which had held these two rivals together. Cæsar's position, too, was rendered precarious by the desperate struggle against the Belgæ, in which he was involved in 53 B.C. In Rome the political pot was boiling furiously. The city was in the grip of the bands of desperadoes hired by Milo and Clodius, who broke up the elections during 53 B.C., so that the first of January, 52, arrived with no chief magistrates in the city. To a man of Curio's daring and versatility this situation offered almost unlimited possibilities, and recognizing this fact, Cicero writes earnestly to him,[128] on the eve of his return, to enlist him in support of Milo's candidacy for the consulship. Curio may have just arrived in the city when matters reached a climax, for on January 18, 52 B.C., Clodius was killed in a street brawl by the followers of Milo, and Pompey was soon after elected sole consul, to bring order out of the chaos, if possible.

Curio was not called upon to support Milo for the consulship, because Milo's share in the murder of Clodius and the elevation of Pompey to his extra-constitutional magistracy put an end to Milo's candidacy. What part he took in supporting or in opposing Pompey's reform legislation of 52 B.C., and what share he had in the preliminary skirmishes between Cæsar and the senate during the early part of 51, we have no means of knowing. As the situation became more acute, however, toward the end of the year, we hear of him again as an active political leader. Cicero's absence from Rome from May, 51 to January, 49 B.C., is a fortunate thing for us, for to it we owe the clever and gossipy political letters which his friend Cælius sent him from the capital. In one of these letters, written August 1, 51 B.C., we learn that Curio is a candidate for the tribunate for the following year, and in it we find a keen analysis of the situation, and an interesting, though tantaizingly brief, estimate of his character. Coming from an intimate friend of Curio, it is especially valuable to us. Cælius writes:[129] "He inspires with great alarm many people who do not know him and do not know how easily he can be influenced, but judging from my hopes and wishes, and from his present behavior, he will prefer to support the Conservatives and the senate. In his present frame of mind he is simply bubbling over with this feeling. The source and reason of this attitude of his lies in the fact that Cæsar, who is in the habit of winning the friendship of men of the worst sort at any cost whatsoever, has shown a great contempt for him. And of the whole affair it seems to me a most delightful outcome, and the view has been taken by the rest, too, to such a degree that Curio, who does nothing after deliberation, seems to have followed a definite policy and definite plans in avoiding the traps of those who had made ready to oppose his election to the tribunate--I mean the Lælii, Antonii, and powerful people of that sort." Without strong convictions or a settled policy, unscrupulous, impetuous, radical, and changeable, these are the qualities which Cælius finds in Curio, and what we have seen of his career leads us to accept the correctness of this estimate. In 61 he had been the champion of Clodius, and the leader of the young Democrats, while two years later we found him the opponent of Cæsar, and an ultra-Conservative. It is in the light of his knowledge of Curio's character, and after receiving this letter from Cælius, that Cicero writes in December, 51 B.C., to congratulate him upon his election to the tribunate. He begs him "to govern and direct his course in all matters in accordance with his own judgment, and not to be carried away by the advice of other people." "I do not fear," he says, "that you may do anything in a fainthearted or stupid way, if you defend those policies which you yourself shall believe to be right.... Commune with yourself, take yourself into counsel, hearken to yourself, determine your own policy."

The other point in the letter of Cælius, his analysis of the political situation, so far as Curio is concerned, is not so easy to follow. Cælius evidently believes that Curio had coquetted with Cæsar and had been snubbed by him, that his intrigues with Cæsar had at first led the aristocracy to oppose his candidacy, but that Cæsar's contemptuous treatment of his advances had driven him into the arms of the senatorial party. It is quite possible, however, that an understanding may have been reached between Cæsar and Curio even at this early date, and that Cæsar's coldness and Curio's conservatism may both have been assumed. This would enable Curio to pose as an independent leader, free from all obligations to Cæsar, Pompey, or the Conservatives, and anxious to see fair play and safeguard the interests of the whole people, an independent leader who was driven over in the end to Cæsar's side by the selfish and factious opposition of the senatorial party to his measures of reform and his advocacy of even-handed justice for both Cæsar and Pompey.[130]

Whether Curio came to an understanding with Cæsar before he entered on his tribunate or not, his policy from the outset was well calculated to make the transfer of his allegiance seem forced upon him, and to help him carry over to Cæsar the support of those who were not blinded by partisan feelings. Before he had been in office a fortnight he brought in a bill which would have annulled the law, passed by Cæsar in his consulship, assigning land in Campania to Pompey's veterans.[131] The repeal of this law had always been a favorite project with the Conservatives, and Curio's proposal seemed to be directed equally against Cæsar and Pompey. In February of 50 B.C. he brought in two bills whose reception facilitated his passage to the Cæsarian party. One of them provided for the repair of the roads, and, as Appian tells us,[132] although "he knew that he could not carry any such measure, he hoped that Pompey's friends would oppose him so that he might have that as an excuse for opposing Pompey." The second measure was to insert an intercalary month. It will be remembered that before Cæsar reformed the calendar, it was necessary to insert an extra month in alternate years, and 50 B.C. was a year in which intercalation was required. Curio's proposal was, therefore, a very proper one. It would recommend itself also on the score of fairness. March 1 had been set as the day on which the senate should take up the question of Cæsar's provinces, and after that date there would be little opportunity to consider other business. Now the intercalated month would have been inserted, in accordance with the regular practice, after February 23, and by its insertion time would have been given for the proper discussion of the measures which Curio had proposed. Incidentally, and probably this was in Curio's mind, the date when Cæsar might be called upon to surrender his provinces would be postponed. The proposal to insert the extra month was defeated, and Curio, blocked in every move by the partisan and unreasonable opposition of Pompey and the Conservatives, found the pretext for which lie had been working, and came out openly for Cæsar.[133] Those who knew him well were not surprised at the transfer of his allegiance. It was probably in fear of such a move that Cicero had urged him not to yield to the influence of others, and when Cicero in Cilicia hears the news, he writes to his friend Cælius: "Is it possible? Curio is now defending Cæsar! Who would have expected it?--except myself, for, as surely as I hope to live, *I* expected it. Heavens! how I miss the laugh we might have had over it." Looking back, as we can now, on the political rôle which Curio played during the next twelve months, it seems strange that two of his intimate friends, who were such far-sighted politicians as Cicero and Cælius were, should have underestimated his political ability so completely. It shows Cæsar's superior political sagacity that he clearly saw his qualities as a leader and tactician. What terms Cæsar was forced to make to secure his support we do not know. Gossip said that the price was sixty million sesterces,[134] or more than two and a half million dollars. He was undoubtedly in great straits. The immense sums which he had spent in celebrating funeral games in honor of his father had probably left him a bankrupt, and large amounts of money were paid for political services during the last years of the republic. Naturally proof of the transaction cannot be had, and even Velleius Paterculus, in his savage arraignment of Curio,[135] does not feel convinced of the truth of the story, but the tale is probable.

It was high time for Cæsar to provide himself with an agent in Rome. The month of March was near at hand, when the long-awaited discussion of his provinces would come up in the senate. His political future, and his rights as a citizen, depended upon his success in blocking the efforts of the senate to take his provinces from him before the end of the year, when he could step from the proconsulship to the consulship. An interval of even a month in private life between the two offices would be all that his enemies would need for bringing political charges against him that would effect his ruin. His displacement before the end of the year must be prevented, therefore, at all hazards. To this task Curio addressed himself, and with surpassing adroitness. He did not come out at once as Cæsar's champion. His function was to hold the scales true between Cæsar and Pompey, to protect the Commonwealth against the overweening ambition and threatening policy of both men. He supported the proposal that Cæsar should be called upon to surrender his army, but coupled with it the demand that Pompey also should be required to give up his troops and his proconsulship. The fairness of his plan appealed to the masses, who would not tolerate a favor to Pompey at Cæsar's expense. It won over even a majority of the senate. The cleverness of his policy was clearly shown at a critical meeting of the senate in December of the year 50 B.C. Appian tells us the story:[136] "In the senate the opinion of each member was asked, and Claudius craftily divided the question and took the votes separately, thus: 'Shall Pompey be deprived of his command?' The majority voted against the latter proposition, and it was decreed that successors to Cæsar should be sent. Then Curio put the question whether both should lay down their commands, and twenty-two voted in the negative, while three hundred and seventy went back to the opinion of Curio in order to avoid civil discord. Then Claudius dismissed the senate, exclaiming: 'Enjoy your victory and have Cæsar for a master!'" The senate's action was vetoed, and therefore had no legal value, but it put Cæsar and Curio in the right and Pompey' s partisans in the wrong.

As a part of his policy of defending Cæsar by calling attention to the exceptional position and the extra-constitutional course of Pompey, Curio offset the Conservative attacks on Cæsar by public speeches fiercely arraigning Pompey for what he had done during his consulship, five years before. When we recall Curio's biting wit and sarcasm, and the unpopularity of Pompey's high-handed methods of that year, we shall appreciate the effectiveness of this flank attack.

Another weapon which he used freely was his unlimited right of veto as tribune. As early as April Cælius appreciated how successful these tactics would be, and he saw the dilemma in which they would put the Conservatives, for he writes to Cicero: "This is what I have to tell you: if they put pressure at every point on Curio, Cæsar will defend his right to exercise the veto; if, as seems likely, they shrink [from overruling him], Cæsar will stay [in his province] as long as he likes." The veto power was the weapon which he used against the senate at the meeting of that body on the first of December, to which reference has already been made. The elections in July had gone against Cæsar. Two Conservatives had been returned as consuls. In the autumn the senate had found legal means of depriving Cæsar of two of his legions. Talk of a compromise was dying down. Pompey, who had been desperately ill in the spring, had regained his strength. He had been exasperated by the savage attacks of Curio. Sensational stories of the movements of Cæsar's troops in the North were whispered in the forum, and increased the tension. In the autumn, for instance, Cæsar had occasion to pay a visit to the towns in northern Italy to thank them for their support of Mark Antony, his candidate for the tribunate, and the wild rumor flew to Rome that he had advanced four legions to Placentia,[137] that his march on the city had begun, and tumult and confusion followed. It was in these circumstances that the consul Marcellus moved in the senate that successors be sent to take over Cæsar's provinces, but the motion was blocked by the veto of Curio, whereupon the consul cried out: "If I am prevented by the vote of the senate from taking steps for the public safety, I will take such steps on my own responsibility as consul." After saying this he darted out of the senate and proceeded to the suburbs with his colleague, where he presented a sword to Pompey, and said: "My colleague and I command you to march against Cæsar in behalf of your country, and we give you for this purpose the army now at Capua, or in any other part of Italy, and whatever additional forces you choose to levy."[138] Curio had accomplished his purpose. He had shown that Pompey as well as Cæsar was a menace to the state; he had prevented Cæsar's recall; he had shown Antony, who was to succeed him in the tribunate, how to exasperate the senate into using coercive measures against his sacrosanct person as tribune and thus justify Cæsar's course in the war, and he had goaded the Conservatives into taking the first overt step in the war by commissioning Pompey to begin a campaign against Cæsar without any authorization from the senate or the people.

The news of the unconstitutional step taken by Marcellus and Pompey reached Rome December 19 or 20. Curio's work as tribune was done, and on the twenty-first of the month he set out for the North to join his leader. The senate would be called together by the new consuls on January 1, and since, before the reform in the calendar, December had only twenty-nine days, there were left only eight days for Curio to reach Cæsar's head-quarters, lay the situation before him, and return to the city with his reply. Ravenna, where Cæsar had his head-quarters, was two hundred and forty miles from Rome. He covered the distance, apparently, in three days, spent perhaps two days with Cæsar, and was back in Rome again for the meeting of the senate on the morning of January 1. Consequently, he travelled at the rate of seventy-five or eighty miles a day, twice the rate of the ordinary Roman courier.

We cannot regret too keenly the fact that we have no account of Curio's meeting with Cæsar, and his recital to Cæsar of the course of events in Rome. In drawing up the document which was prepared at this conference, Cæsar must have been largely influenced by the intimate knowledge which Curio had of conditions in the capital, and of the temper of the senate. It was an ultimatum, and, when

Curio presented it to the senate, that body accepted the challenge, and called upon Cæsar to lay down his command on a specified date or be declared a public enemy. Cæsar replied by crossing the border of his province and occupying one town after another in northern Italy in rapid succession. All this had been agreed upon in the meeting between Curio and Cæsar, and Velleius Paterculus[139] is probably right in putting the responsibility for the war largely on the shoulders of Curio, who, as he says, brought to naught the fair terms of peace which Cæsar was ready to propose and Pompey to accept. The whole situation points to the conclusion that Cæsar did not desire war, and was not prepared for it. Had he anticipated its immediate outbreak, he would scarcely have let it arise when he had only one legion with him on the border, while his other ten legions were a long distance away.

From the outset Curio took an active part in the war which he had done so much to bring about, and it was an appropriate thing that the closing events in his life should have been recorded for us by his great patron, Cæsar, in his narrative of the Civil War. On the 18th or 19th of January, within ten days of the crossing of the Rubicon, we hear of his being sent with a body of troops to occupy Iguvium,[140] and a month later he is in charge of one of the investing camps before the stronghold of Corfinium.[141] With the fall of Corfinium, on the 21st of February, Cæsar's rapid march southward began, which swept the Pompeians out of Italy within a month and gave Cæsar complete control of the peninsula. In that brilliant campaign Curio undoubtedly took an active part, for at the close of it Cæsar gave him an independent commission for the occupation of Sicily and northern Africa. No more important command could have been given him, for Sicily and Africa were the granaries of Rome, and if the Pompeians continued to hold them, the Cæsarians in Italy might be starved into submission. To this ill-fated campaign Cæsar devotes the latter half of the second book of his Civil War. In the beginning of his account of it he remarks: "Showing at the outset a total contempt for the military strength of his opponent, Publius Attius Varus, Curio crossed over from Sicily, accompanied by only two of the four legions originally given him by Cæsar, and by only five hundred cavalry."[142] The estimate which Cælius had made of him was true, after all, at least in military affairs. He was bold and impetuous, and lacked a settled policy. Where daring and rapidity of movement could accomplish his purpose, he succeeded, but he lacked patience in finding out the size and disposition of the enemy's forces and calmness of judgment in comparing his own strength with that of his foe. It was this weakness in his character as a military leader which led him to join battle with Varus and Juba's lieutenant, Saburra, without learning beforehand, as he might have done, that Juba, with a large army, was encamped not six miles in the rear of Saburra. Curio's men were surrounded by the enemy and cut down as they stood. His staff begged him to seek safety in flight, but, as Cæsar writes,[143] "He answered without hesitation that, having lost the army which Cæsar had entrusted to his charge, he would never return to look him in the face, and with that answer he died fighting."

Three years later the fortunes of war brought Cæsar to northern Africa, and he traversed a part of the region where Curio's luckless campaign had been carried on. With the stern eye of the trained soldier, he marked the fatal blunders which Curio had made, but he recalled also the charm of his personal qualities, and the defeat before Utica was forgotten in his remembrance of the great victory which Curio had won for him, single-handed, in Rome. Even Lucan, a partisan of the senate which Curio had flouted, cannot withhold his admiration for Curio's brilliant career, and his pity for Curio's tragic end. As he stands in imagination before the fallen Roman leader, he exclaims:[144] "Happy wouldst thou be, O Rome, and destined to bless thy people, had it pleased the gods above to guard thy liberty as it pleased them to avenge its loss. Lo! the noble body of Curio, covered by no tomb, feeds the birds of Libya. But to thee, since it profiteth not to pass in silence those deeds of thine which their own glory defends forever 'gainst the decay of time, such tribute now we pay, O youth, as thy life has well deserved. No other citizen of such talent has Rome brought forth, nor one to whom the law would be indebted more, if he the path of right had followed out. As it was, the corruption of the age ruined the city when desire for office, pomp, and the power which wealth gives, ever to be dreaded, had swept away his wavering mind with sidelong flood, and the change of Curio, snared by the spoils of Gaul and the gold of Cæsar, was that which turned the tide of history. Although mighty Sulla, fierce Marius, the blood-bespattered Cinna, and all the line of Cæsar's house have held our throats at their mercy with the sword, to whom was e'er such power vouchsafed? All others bought, *he* sold the state."

## Gaius Matius, a Friend of Cæsar

*"Non enim Cæsarem ... sum secutus, sed amicum."*

Gaius Matius, the subject of this sketch, was neither a great warrior, nor statesman, nor writer. If his claim to remembrance rested on what he did in the one or the other of these rôles, he would long ago have been forgotten. It is his genius for friendship which has kept his memory green, and that is what he himself would have wished. Of his early life we know little, but it does not matter much, because the interest which he has for us centres about his relations to Cæsar in early manhood. Being of good birth, and a man of studious tastes, he probably attended the University at Athens, and heard lectures there as young Cicero and Messala did at a later period. He must have been a man of fine tastes and cultivation, for Cicero, in writing to a friend, bestows on Matius the title "doctissimus," the highest literary compliment which one Roman could pay another, and Apollodorus of Pergamum dedicated to him his treatise on rhetoric. Since he was born about 84 B.C., he returned from his years of study at Athens about the time when Cæsar was setting out on his brilliant campaign in Gaul. Matius joined him, attracted perhaps by the personal charms of the young proconsul, perhaps by the love of adventure, perhaps, like his friend Trebatius, by the hope of making a reputation.

At all events he was already with Cæsar somewhere in Gaul in 53 B.C., and it is hard to think of an experience better suited to lay bare the good and the bad qualities in Cæsar's character than the years of camp life which Matius spent with him in the wilds of Gaul and Britain. As aide-de-camp, or orderly, for such a position he probably held, his place was by Cæsar's side. They forded the rivers together, walked or rode through woodland or open side by side, shared the same meagre rations, and lay in the same tent at the end of the day's march, ready to spring from the ground at a moment's warning to defend each other against attack from the savage foe. Cæsar's narrative of his campaigns in Gaul is a soldier's story of military movements, and perhaps from our school-boy remembrance of it we may have as little a liking for it as Horace had for the poem of Livius Andronicus, which he studied under "Orbilius of the rods," but even the obscurities of the Latin subjunctive and ablative cannot have blinded us entirely to the romance of the desperate siege of Alesia and the final struggle which the Gauls made to drive back the invader. Matius shared with Cæsar all the hardships and perils of that campaign, and with Cæsar he witnessed the final scene of the tragedy when Vercingetorix, the heroic Gallic chieftain, gave up his sword, and the conquest of Gaul was finished. It is little wonder that

Matius and the other young men who followed Cæsar were filled with admiration of the man who had brought all this to pass.

It was a notable group, including Trebatius, Hirtius, Pansa, Oppius, and Matius in its number. All of them were of the new Rome. Perhaps they were dimly conscious that the mantle of Tiberius Gracchus had fallen upon their leader, that the great political struggle which had been going on for nearly a century was nearing its end, and that they were on the eve of a greater victory than that at Alesia. It would seem that only two of them, Matius and Trebatius, lived to see the dawning of the new day. But it was not simply nor mainly the brilliancy of Cæsar as a leader in war or in politics which attracted Matius to him. As he himself puts it in his letter to Cicero: "I did not follow a Cæsar, but a friend." Lucullus and Pompey had made as distinguished a record in the East as Cæsar had in the West, but we hear of no such group of able young men following their fortunes as attached themselves to Cæsar. We must find a reason for the difference in the personal qualities of Cæsar, and there is nothing that more clearly proves the charm of his character than the devotion to him of this group of men. In the group Matius is the best representative of the man and the friend. When Cæsar came into his own, Matius neither asked for nor accepted the political offices which Cæsar would gladly have given him. One needs only to recall the names of Antony, Labienus, or Decimus Brutus to realize the fact that Cæsar remembered and rewarded the faithful services of his followers. But Matius was Cæsar's friend and nothing more, not his master of the horse, as Antony was, nor his political and financial heir, as Octavius was. In his loyalty to Cæsar he sought for no other reward than Cæsar's friendship, and his services to him brought with them their own return. Indeed, through his friend he suffered loss, for one of Cæsar's laws robbed him of a part of his estate, as he tells us, but this experience did not lessen his affection. How different his attitude was from that of others who professed a friendship for Cæsar! Some of them turned upon their leader and plotted against his life, when disappointed in the favors which they had received at his hands, and others, when he was murdered, used his name and his friendship for them to advance their own ambitious designs. Antony and Octavius struggle with each other to catch the reins of power which have fallen from his hands; Dolabella, who seems to regard himself as an understudy of Cæsar, plays a serio-comic part in Rome in his efforts to fill the place of the dead dictator; while Decimus Brutus hurries to the North to make sure of the province which Cæsar had given him.

From these men, animated by selfishness, by jealousy, by greed for gain, by sentimentalism, or by hypocritical patriotism, Matius stands aloof, and stands perhaps alone. For him the death of Cæsar means the loss of a friend, of a man in whom he believed. He can find no common point of sympathy either with those who rejoice in the death of the tyrant, as Cicero does, for he had not thought Cæsar a tyrant, nor with those who use the name of Cæsar to conjure with. We have said that he accepted no political office. He did accept an office, that of procurator, or superintendent, of the public games which Cæsar had vowed on the field of Pharsalus, but which death had stepped in to prevent him from giving, and it was in the pious fulfilment of this duty which he took upon himself that he brought upon his head the anger of the "auctores libertatis," as he ironically calls them. He had grieved, too, at the death of Cæsar, although "a man ought to rate the fatherland above a friend," as the liberators said. Matius took little heed of this talk. He had known of it from the outset, but it had not troubled him. Yet when it came to his ears that his friend Cicero, to whom he had been attached from boyhood, to whom he had proved his fidelity at critical moments, was among his accusers, he could not but complain bitterly of the injustice. Through a common friend, Trebatius, whose acquaintance he had made in Gaul, he expresses to Cicero the sorrow which he feels at his unkindness. What Cicero has to say in explanation of his position and in defence of himself, we can do no better than to give in his own words:

"*Cicero to Matins, greeting:*[145]

"I am not yet quite clear in my own mind whether our friend Trebatius, who is as loyal as he is devoted to both of us, has brought me more sorrow or pleasure: for I reached my Tusculan villa in the evening, and the next day, early in the morning, he came to see me, though he had not yet recovered his strength. When I reproved him for giving too little heed to his health, he said that nothing was nearer his heart than seeing me. 'There's nothing new,' say I? He told me of your grievance against me, yet before I make any reply in regard to it, let me state a few facts.

"As far back as I can recall the past I have no friend of longer standing than you are; but long duration is a thing characteristic of many friendships, while love is not. I loved you on the day I met you, and I believed myself loved by you. Your subsequent departure, and that too for a long time, my electoral canvass, and our different modes of life did not allow our inclination toward one another to be strengthened by intimacy; still I saw your feeling toward me many years before the Civil War, while Cæsar was in Gaul; for the result which you thought would be of great advantage to me and not of disadvantage to Cæsar himself you accomplished: I mean in bringing him to love me, to honor me, to regard me as one of his friends. Of the many confidential communications which passed between us in those days, by word of mouth, by letter, by message, I say nothing, for sterner times followed. At the breaking out of the Civil War, when you were on your way toward Brundisium to join Cæsar, you came to me to my Formian villa. In the first place, how much did that very fact mean, especially at those times! Furthermore, do you think I have forgotten your counsel, your words, the kindness you showed? I remember that Trebatius was there. Nor indeed have I forgotten the letter which you sent to me after meeting Cæsar, in the district near Trebula, as I remember it. Next came that ill-fated moment when either my regard for public opinion, or my sense of duty, or chance, call it what you will, compelled me to go to Pompey. What act of kindness or thoughtfulness either toward me in my absence or toward my dear ones in Rome did you neglect? In fact, whom have all my friends thought more devoted to me and to themselves than you are? I came to Brundisium. Do you think I have forgotten in what haste, as soon as you heard of it, you came hurrying to me from Tarentum? How much your presence meant to me, your words of cheer to a courage broken by the fear of universal disaster! Finally, our life at Rome began. What element did our friendship lack? In most important matters I followed your advice with reference to my relations toward Cæsar; in other matters I followed my own sense of duty. With whom but myself, if Cæsar be excepted, have you gone so far as to visit his house again and again, and to spend there many hours, oftentimes in the most delightful discourse? It was then too, if you remember, that you persuaded me to write those philosophical essays of mine. After his return, what purpose was more in your thoughts than to have me as good a friend of Cæsar as possible? This you accomplished at once.

"What is the point, then, of this discourse, which is longer than I had intended it should be? This is the point, that I have been surprised that you, who ought to see these things, have believed that I have taken any step which is out of harmony with our friendly relations, for beside these facts which I have mentioned, which are undisputed and self-evident facts, there are many more intimate ties of friendship which I can scarcely put in words. Everything about you charms me, but most of all, on the one hand, your perfect loyalty in matters of friendship, your wisdom, dignity, steadfastness; on the other hand, your wit, refinement, and literary tastes.

"Wherefore--now I come back to the grievance--in the first place, I did not think that you had voted for that law; in the second place, if I had thought so, I should never have thought that you had done it without some sufficient reason. Your position makes whatever you do noticeable; furthermore, envy puts some of your acts in a worse light than the facts warrant. If you do not hear these rumors I do not know what to say. So far as I am concerned, if I ever hear them I defend you as I know that *I* am always defended by *you* against *my* detractors. And my defence follows two lines: there are some things which I always deny *in toto*, as, for instance, the statement in regard to that very vote; there are other acts of yours which I maintain were dictated by considerations of affection and kindness, as, for instance, your action with reference to the management of the games. But it does not escape you, with all your wisdom, that, if Cæsar was a king--which seems to me at any rate to have been the case--with respect of your duty two positions may be maintained, either the one which I am in the habit of taking, that your loyalty and friendship to Cæsar are to be praised, or the one which some people take, that the freedom of one's fatherland is to be esteemed more than the life of one's friend. I wish that my discussions springing out of these conversations had been repeated to you.

"Indeed, who mentions either more gladly or more frequently than I the two following facts, which are especially to your honor? The fact that you were the most influential opponent of the Civil War, and that you were the most earnest advocate of temperance in the moment of victory, and in this matter I have found no one to disagree with me. Wherefore I am grateful to our friend Trebatius for giving me an opportunity to write this letter, and if you are not convinced by it, you will think me destitute of all sense of duty and kindness; and nothing more serious to me than that or more foreign to your own nature can happen."

In all the correspondence of Cicero there is not a letter written with more force and delicacy of feeling, none better suited to accomplish its purpose than this letter to Matius. It is a work of art; but in that fact lies its defect, and in that respect it is in contrast to the answer which it called forth from Matius, The reply of Matius stands on a level with another better-known non-Ciceronian epistle, the famous letter of condolence which Servius wrote to Cicero after the death of Cicero's daughter, Tullia; but it is finer, for, while Servius is stilted and full of philosophical platitudes, Matius, like Shakespeare's Antony, "only speaks right on," in telling Cicero of his grief at Cæsar's death, of his indignation at the intolerant attitude of the assassins, and his determination to treasure the memory of Cæsar at any cost. This is his letter:

"*Matius to Cicero, greeting*[146]

"I derived great pleasure from your letter, because I saw that you held such an opinion about me as I had hoped you would hold, and wished you to hold; and although, in regard to that opinion, I had no misgivings, still, inasmuch as I considered it a matter of the greatest importance, I was anxious that it should continue unchanged. And then I was conscious of having done nothing to offend any good citizen; therefore I was the less inclined to believe that you, endowed as you are with so many excellent qualities, could be influenced by any idle rumors, especially as my friendship toward you had been and was sincere and unbroken. Since I know that matters stand in this respect as I have wished them to stand, I will reply to the charges, which you have often refuted in my behalf in such a way as one would expect from that kindness of heart characteristic of you and from our friendship. It is true that what men said against me after the death of Cæsar was known to me. They call it a sin of mine that I sorrow over the death of a man dear to me, and because I grieve that he whom I loved is no more, for they say that 'fatherland should be above friendship,' just as if they had proved already that his death has been of service to the state. But I will make no subtle plea. I confess that I have not attained to your high philosophic planes; for, on the one hand, in the Civil War I did not follow a Cæsar, but a friend, and although I was grieved at the state of things, still I did not desert him; nor, on the other hand, did I at any time approve of the Civil War, nor even of the reason for strife, which I most earnestly sought to extinguish when it was kindling. Therefore, in the moment of victory for one bound to me by the closest ties, I was not captivated by the charm either of public office or of gold, while his other friends, although they had less influence with him than I, misused these rewards in no small degree. Nay, even my own property was impaired by a law of Cæsar's, thanks to which very law many who rejoice at the death of Cæsar have remained at Rome.

I have worked as for my own welfare that conquered citizens might be spared.

"Then may not I, who have desired the welfare of all, be indignant that he, from whom this favor came, is dead? especially since the very men who were forgiven have brought him both unpopularity and death. You shall be punished, then, they say, 'since you dare to disapprove of our deed.' Unheard of arrogance, that some men glory in their crime, that others may not even sorrow over it without punishment! But it has always been the unquestioned right, even of slaves, to fear, to rejoice, to grieve according to the dictates of their own feelings rather than at the bidding of another man; of these rights, as things stand now, to judge from what these champions of freedom keep saying, they are trying to deprive us by intimidation; but their efforts are useless. I shall never be driven by the terrors of any danger from the path of duty or from the claims of friendship, for I have never thought that a man should shrink from an honorable death; nay, I have often thought that he should seek it. But why are they angry at me, if I wish them to repent of their deed? for I desire to have Cæsar's death a bitter thing to all men.

"'But I ought as a citizen to desire the welfare of the state.' Unless my life in the past and my hope for the future, without words from me, prove that I desire that very end, I do not seek to establish the fact by words. Wherefore I beg you the more earnestly to consider deeds more than words, and to believe, if you feel that it is well for the right to prevail, that I can have no intercourse with dishonorable men. For am I now, in my declining years, to change that course of action which I maintained in my youth, when I might even have gone astray with hope of indulgence, and am I to undo my life's work? I will not do so. Yet I shall take no step which may be displeasing to any man, except to grieve at the cruel fate of one most closely bound to me, of one who was a most illustrious man. But if I were otherwise minded, I would never deny what I was doing lest I should be regarded as shameless in doing wrong, a coward and a hypocrite in concealing it.

"'Yet the games which the young Cæsar gave in memory of Cæsar's victory I superintended.' But that has to do with my private obligation and not with the condition of the state; a duty, however, which I owed to the memory and the distinguished position of a dear friend even though he was dead, a duty which I could not decline when asked by a young man of most excellent promise and most worthy of Cæsar. 'I even went frequently to the house of the consul Antony to pay my respects!' to whom you will find that those who think that I am lacking in devotion to my country kept coming in throngs to ask some favor forsooth or secure some reward. But what arrogance this is that, while Cæsar never interfered with my cultivating the friendship of men whom I pleased, even when he himself did not like them, these men who have taken my friend from me should try to prevent me by their slander from loving those whom I will.

"But I am not afraid lest the moderation of my life may prove too weak to withstand false reports, or that even those who do not love me because of my loyalty to Cæsar may not prefer to have friends like me rather than like themselves. So far as I myself am concerned, if what I prefer shall be my lot, the life which is left me I shall spend in retirement at Rhodes; but if some untoward circumstance shall prevent it, I shall live at Rome in such a wise as to desire always that right be done. Our friend Trebatius I thank heartily in that he has disclosed your sincere and friendly feeling toward me, and has shown me that him whom I have always loved of my own free will I ought with the more reason to esteem and honor. Bene vale et me dilige."

With these words our knowledge of Matius comes almost to an end. His life was prolonged into the imperial period, and, strangely enough, in one of the few references to him which we find at a later date, he is characterized as "the friend of Augustus" (divi Augusti amicus). It would seem that the affection which he felt for Cæsar he transferred to Cæsar's heir and successor. He still holds no office or title. In this connection it is interesting to recall the fact that we owe the best of Cicero's philosophical work to him, the "Academics," the "De Finibus," and the "Tusculan Questions," for Cicero tells us in his letter that he was induced to write his treatises on philosophy by Matius. It is a pleasant thing to think that to him we may also be indebted for Cicero's charming essay "On Friendship." The later life of Matius, then, we may think was spent in retirement, in the study of philosophy, and in the pursuit of literature. His literary pursuits give a homely and not unpleasant touch to his character. They were concerned with gastronomy, for Columella, in the first century of our era, tells us[147] that Matius composed three books, bearing the titles of "The Cook," "The Butler," and "The Picklemaker," and his name was transmitted to a later generation in a dish known as "mincemeat à la Matius" (*minutal Matianum*).[148] He passes out of the pages of history in the writings of Pliny the Elder as the man who "invented the practice of clipping shrubbery."[149] To him, then, we perhaps owe the geometrical figures, and the forms of birds and beasts which shrubs take in the modern English garden. His memory is thus ever kept green, whether in a way that redounds to his credit or not is left for the reader to decide.

## Index

Wages in Roman times; compared with to-day; and guilds; and slavery. (See also *Salaries*.)

Printed in the United Kingdom
by Lightning Source UK Ltd.
112627UKS00001B/105

9 781406 503548